THE CURIOUS CASE OF BINAYAK SEN

Dilip D'Souza is a writer based in Bombay, though there was a time when he wrote software in the USA. He has won several awards for his writing, including, most recently, the Newsweek/ Daily Beast Open Hands Prize for Commentary (2012). He has written three books, the last one being *Roadrunner: An Indian Quest in America*.

THE CURIOUS CASE OF BINAYAK SEN

DILIP D'SOUZA

HarperCollins *Publishers* India

First published in India in 2012 by
HarperCollins *Publishers* India

Building 10, Tower A, 4th Floor, DLF Cyber City, Phase II,
Gurugram Haryana – 122002, India
www.harpercollins.co.in

2 4 6 8 10 9 7 5 3 1

ISBN: 978-93-5029-486-4

Typeset in 11/ 14.3 Cochin LT Std
InoSoft Systems Noida

Printed and bound at
MicroPrints india, New Delhi

For V, who believes in me, and for R&R, who inspire me

AUTHOR DISCLAIMER

I use the words 'Naxalite' and 'Maoist' as equivalents in this book. Not that they are necessarily so, but this is now such a commonly used convenience that it would be self-consciously artificial to make a distinction.

Contents

1	A Way of Thinking	1
2	Surrounded by Promise	8
3	Rural Hospital	16
4	Interlude: About Two Girls	29
5	Man of the 21st	33
6	The Case	60
7	Charge sheets and Sheets	70
8	Insinuation	82
9	Interlude: What Development Means	87
10	Look at the Evidence	97
11	Interlude: So Says the Chart	113
12	Judgement	119
13	Interlude: Prisoners	135
14	Sedition	141
15	Implications	150
16	Doctor Only in Name	169
17	A Commentary	177
	Notes	180
	Appendix 1: Timeline	185
	Acknowledgements	187

1

A Way of Thinking

How do you begin to understand a man like Binayak Sen? This is no naïve question. Consider that Sen is a doctor. Consider what that means.

Even today, the medical profession remains an attractive career option to thousands of hopeful young Indians. It brings both money and respect. If you think of the doctors you know, who have treated you over the years, you will understand what I am saying. It's likely you remember them as men and women of character and intellect, of some standing in the community, certainly among their peers. Doctors do well for themselves, financially and otherwise, in our cities and elsewhere.

How then do you comprehend Sen? He chose a path different from those that other doctors tread, giving up the financial gains and urban comforts that most of them enjoy. Instead, Sen lived and worked in rural India, among some of the world's most neglected people. He treated them for a range of diseases, from elephantiasis to filariasis. He built a reputation for himself, not among people who might write and talk about him, but among those who have limited access to doctors and medicine.

This is not to paint some glowing picture of heroism in action. That's not a pursuit that interests me. Having met him, I know it doesn't interest Sen either. But I do admire Sen for reaching a place few of us find in our lives: he makes a living doing what he wants, on his own terms, and as it turns out, it's what he was trained to do.

How many of us can say the same about ourselves? This is why it is worth making an effort to understand Sen.

For me, it was less of an effort than I might have imagined. I know a doctor couple who have spent over two decades in work and circumstances similar to Sen's. Watching them closely in that time has given me a perspective on and an appreciation for what drives them.

It's not money. They don't live frugally, but by no means are they extravagant in their tastes either. And they continue to do what they have done all these years, what they were trained to do: preventive health care.

What then motivates this couple? I think there's a simple answer: they just wanted to work with India's poorest. They wanted to make a difference. They relish the challenge of preventive, as opposed to curative, health care. They crave the job satisfaction that comes from doing something that's called 'meaningful'. They believe the medical profession is noble because its practitioners serve fellow human beings;

and that because of their circumstances, some people are in greater need of health care than others.

And I repeat, these words are not meant to put this couple on a pedestal and call them modern-day heroes. Like with Sen, they have their convictions, but this is also their work. That combination has always struck me as rare.

I also think people like Sen and this doctor couple were shaped by circumstances that you don't easily find today, in the India of the twenty-first century. These are children of the first post-Independence generation. They were untouched by the blight of British rule, but touched nevertheless by tales of the euphoria their parents felt on that day in August 1947. They grew up in an India still charged with the optimism of freedom. As young adults, they were conscious of being a part of something larger than themselves, this great experiment in building a nation.

Bertrand Russell captured some of that early Indian spirit I am trying to allude to here. In 1959, BBC Radio interviewed Russell. The discussion turned to nationalism and the countries around the world that had recently become independent. Russell spoke about what happens when oppressed people free themselves. 'As soon as they get free,' he said, 'they devote themselves ... to practicing all the vices that previously were practiced by their oppressors'. It was a time of decolonization, and Russell must have had in mind countries like Tanzania, the Congo or Vietnam, all of which descended into chaos and civil war after they won independence.

Russell's BBC interviewer asked: 'Is this an inevitable pattern?'

'No, no!' exclaimed Russell. 'It's not inevitable, and it doesn't always happen. I think one must take India as a case of how it doesn't always happen. I think India, since it became free, has been singularly without that sort of vice which so often happens to liberated people.'

Russell's words are simultaneously an acknowledgement of and a tribute to an India trying to find a different way in the world, a sign that enough people recognized and appreciated that attempt. After all, men of uncommon morals, intellect and vision led India in those early years. They fired an entire country with their ideals, energy and the conviction that there was no challenge – health, education, poverty, disease or social ills – that we could not address and overcome.

Such was the climate in the country even a decade after the British left, years before the cynicism and corruption of later decades. Arguably, this mood that Russell referred to lasted till our first prime minister, Jawaharlal Nehru, died in 1964.

And such was the climate into which Sen was born, in 1951. The doctor couple I mentioned earlier, born in 1958 and 1963, also belong to this first post-Independence generation. Many among them grew up believing they owed something to their fellow Indians. Like their parents, they believed public service was one of the best things they could do with their lives.

My father, who joined the Indian Administrative Service (IAS) at the time of Independence and had a long and fascinating career in the service, was one such parent. He spent a fair fraction of my growing-up years trying to persuade me to join the bureaucracy. In my youth, this made no sense to me: how could there be anything interesting or glamorous in a career working for the government? But his point was simple: if I at all wanted to make a difference, however small, the IAS was the place to do it in the most interesting and fulfilling way. According to him, if I was inclined towards public service, no job could ever be more absorbing. Yet I always felt this was some peculiar joke. Years older now – and too old to appear for the IAS exam – I know he was not joking. I understand now what he was getting at. I should have taken him seriously.

This is what public service meant, in those early decades.

Sen's career path and the choices he made fit this worldview; they were also of a piece with other children of that time that I knew well. For example, and referring to doctors in particular, even I knew of community health as a desirable and prestigious subject MBBS graduates might choose to study for their MD degree. This was because the course trained you to work in rural India, to deal with the concerns of Indians who had poor access to health care, and this was something worth doing. It was worth doing because of the need and the satisfaction, which compensated for any shortfall in salaries.

I remember one such doctor pointing me to a study that showed that the average distance an Indian tribal walked to reach a basic health care facility was six kilometres (as opposed to much smaller distances for urban Indians). She showed it to me as if to say, 'Now you understand why I am doing this.' Such doctors were motivated to confront such Indian realities, and trained to address and maybe even solve them.

Sen, I've always felt, was one more such doctor. I did not know him when he was growing up. But it did not surprise me to learn, when I first got to know about him, that he was a doctor working in rural India. His was a generation in which young men and women chose that kind of career and valued it. And this is why understanding Sen meant visiting two places that shaped his career and thought: the college where he learned his trade, and the hospital he worked at early in his career.

Of course, other places would also say a lot about the man – his school, his neighbourhood, the clinic he ran in rural Chhattisgarh. But writing about those would turn this into a biography, which I don't want. More than his life, my interest, for this book, lies in the legal case against Sen.

I believe this is a case against not just a man but an entire thought process. It has to do with a certain concern for your fellow humans in less privileged circumstances than you. It has to do with questioning. It has to do with the recognition that in a complex world, issues and answers are not black-and-white, not yes or no, but necessarily complex – and that is ok. It has to do with a faith in the way institutions function, or must function, and the determination to hold them to that standard. It has to do with the assumption we all make about our system of justice, almost an article of faith: that if you accuse someone of a serious crime, you had better produce equally serious evidence to support your accusation. 'There can be no smoke without a fire' is fine as far as it goes, but there comes a time when we had better see the fire for ourselves, or the smoke itself is suspect.

It has to do with respect for the law, without assuming infallibility in the process of law. That sentence is not one long oxymoron; in fact, I would argue that respect assumes fallibility, and therefore a chance to redeem and improve.

For these reasons, this is really not a book about Sen, this one man. It is instead about his way of thinking about the world. And if his college – the Christian Medical College in Vellore – and hospital – the Shaheed Hospital in Dalli-Rajhara – helped shape that thinking, I wanted to know about them.

2

Surrounded by Promise

About a generation ago, the great Indian middle class conundrum was whether your kids should study engineering or medicine at college. There were those who aspired to study law, or economics at St. Stephen's College ('Stephen's Eco'), but they were the exceptions. And I don't remember anyone in my high school class speaking of the IAS. The hoi polloi like me tried to decide between the two main streams. Our choice was often decided by how well we did at biology, though I still don't know if a flair for biology is any kind of indicator of prowess as a doctor. But anyway, that was how some of us made up our minds. I preferred mathematics, so I ended up in an engineering college.

The biology-philes had a list of medical schools they aspired to join, their acronyms forming a kind of alphabet-soup that grew familiar even to us non-aspirants. We would hear of AFMC (the Armed Forces Medical College in Pune), AIIMS (the All India Institute of Medical Sciences,

New Delhi), JIPMER (the Jawaharlal Institute of Postgraduate Medical Education and Research, Pondicherry), CMC (the Christian Medical College, Vellore) and St John's, Bangalore. Each of these institutions had its own difficult entrance examination. In my high school years, a boy a couple of years senior to me got through the AIIMS exam and left for Delhi to become a doctor. Already known as one of the better students in his class, this only served to confirm his pedigree. I still remember the awe we all felt.

CMC was equally awe-inspiring. It remains one of the country's – arguably one of the world's – premier training grounds for doctors. It also offers a greatly respected postgraduate degree in community health. MDs from that programme are found in hospitals in rural Orissa, Tamil Nadu, Madhya Pradesh and elsewhere.

In some ways, this is really the legacy of the legendary woman who founded CMC, Ida Scudder. Since her vision and resolve still seem to be part of a CMC education, I asked Dr P. Zachariah, long-time professor of physiology at CMC and 'PZach' to generations of students, to tell me about Ida.

Ida Scudder came from a family of 'medical missionaries' of the Reformed Church of America. Her grandfather, John Scudder, was one of the first medical missionaries in Southeast Asia, and started a hospital in Sri Lanka early in the nineteenth century. Later, he came to India and was the first medical missionary in this country. His youngest son, John Jr, was Ida's father.

By the time Ida was born in 1870, there was already a long family tradition of service steeped in Christianity. Yet the story goes that Ida herself was not enamoured of being a missionary in India and was looking forward to studying and settling down in her home country, the US. Until, just before she left for college in America, she came face to face with some realities of India, this other home country where she had grown up. One night, she heard that there were three women in labour. Since they didn't want a man to help with their deliveries, they asked if Ida would come. For whatever reason, Ida did not respond. The three women died.

This possibly apocryphal tragedy was, in Zachariah's telling, an 'epiphany' for Ida Scudder. It decided the course of her life. She went to the US, studied medicine at Cornell University, and returned to India at the dawn of the new century to start a clinic for women and children in Vellore. Over the next decade, she not only treated thousands of women, but also trained what we would today call village health workers or auxiliary nurse-midwives (ANMs). She understood that if she had to deliver health care to rural India, some level of care would have to come from such workers; many rural clinics follow the same model even today.

By 1918, Ida knew she would have to start training full-fledged doctors too. She therefore decided to open a medical college for girls. She was widely scorned for this daft idea: women, and training to be doctors? Upper-class Indians would never send their daughters to her, people said. She'd be lucky to get even a few applicants, people said. Where would the girls stay, who would teach them?

Ida promised parents that their daughters would stay with her, and that proved persuasive. The story goes that she had over 150 applicants in the first year. She selected twenty, of whom eighteen graduated. Thus was CMC born.

Over the years, the college grew in strength. In 1949, it began admitting men – there were ten in a class of thirty-five. In 1955, admissions increased to fifty, and then to the current level of sixty in the early 1960s. Twenty-five seats are still reserved for women, but typically two-thirds of the students are women. The college is now considering raising admissions to 100 every year.

CMC has always encouraged a close relationship between faculty and students. I've sensed this in all the CMC graduates I've known, and PZach confirmed it. Each incoming student is assigned a faculty member who mentors him or her through the years in college. The college has also always encouraged a hands-on engagement with broader health care issues, and not just in the CMC hospital. So, as part of their curriculum, students do three stints at one of fifteen 'peripheral' hospitals around India. 'We want them to see how their clinical work is socially relevant to the community', PZach told me.

This can mean all kinds of things, of course. One place to get a sense of this idea of social relevance is a CMC initiative called the Low Cost Effective Care Unit (LCECU). Sara Bhattacharji, another long-time CMC professor, is on the LCECU team. On an evening that threatened rain in Vellore, she spoke to me at length about the unit and gave me a booklet, *Ripples of Life*, which was published to mark its silver jubilee in 2008.

LCECU is located in the CMC hospital's 'Scudder Ward', actually on the spot where Ida Scudder established her original clinic. It is now in the middle of a slum area in the heart of Vellore, and for a reason. It is dedicated 'to the health needs of the shifting, impoverished population that calls these areas home', reads the booklet. But just as important, the booklet says, is the way LCECU is 'philosophically located'. Meaning the way it relates to the community around it:

> 'In responding to the health needs of the community, its staff believe passionately in the importance of a genuine, personal engagement in the realities of people's lives and the priority of exposing young trainee health professionals to those realities.'[1]

In other words, and this is a theme that will echo through this book, health care must be about more than treating illness and disease. It has to also consider wider issues. Take for instance the story Bhattacharji told me about Ranjit (also recounted in *Ripples of Life*).

Ranjit was nineteen when his alcoholic father died. Being the oldest of four siblings, he was suddenly responsible for the whole family. He kept his brothers in school and decided to get his sister married. As often happens in Tamil Nadu, the groom he had in mind was a maternal uncle. Ranjit hoped that the marriage would mean the uncle would help take care of the family. Except that his sister had a boyfriend closer to her own age, and married him instead. Infuriated, Ranjit cut off all contact with her.

Soon after, he began suffering serious pain in his abdomen. Initially, the doctors at LCECU could not diagnose his condition, and it worsened. Then he started bleeding from the rectum. There was a tumour in his colon. *Ripples of Life* tells us: 'Beside himself with fear and anger, Ranjit tore up his hospital notes and took himself home. 'You have ruined my life!' he shouted.'

But Ranjit needed treatment, a colostomy and palliative care. It was obvious: he was dying. Staff from the unit visited him regularly and eventually learned about his estranged sister. They persuaded him to reach out and reconcile with her. After he did that, she moved with her family to Ranjit's home and took care of him. 'Ranjit died', I read in *Ripples of Life*, 'having made peace with himself and with the world.'

Who would have imagined that training to become a doctor might involve learning about the tensions in a patient's family, and trying to address them? Ranjit died, yes, but who can put a value on having his sister at home in his last weeks, taking care of him? This is an instance of what CMC is about.

After Ranjit's story, the LCECU booklet offers some questions for discussion. Here are two:

- What is the responsibility of the health care worker when the illness is no longer curable and the patient is dying?
- What resources exist in a community to deal with terminal illness, dying and death?

Reading *Ripples of Life*, and hearing about LCECU, underlines the emphasis CMC places on the community and looking beyond immediately applicable drugs and treatment.

But according to Sara Bhattacharji, it is harder to impart this wider view of medicine to students today than it was a generation ago. Today, there's a far greater focus on the individual, be it achievement or responsibility. For students, it's about 'I': I do things primarily for myself, I am responsible primarily for myself, it's not necessarily a virtue to be concerned about the world around me. And yet CMC is persistent in its commitment to produce doctors who are attuned to the larger issues.

Binayak Sen joined CMC in 1967. In those years when he was in college in Vellore, India was still a young nation, one in ferment in all kinds of ways. Indira Gandhi had become prime minister the year before, having broken ranks with the jaded Congress politicians of her father's generation. Five years later in 1971, she led the country through the memorable liberation of Bangladesh, an achievement to make India proud and, possibly, her finest moment as prime minister. Elsewhere in the world, 1968 was a watershed year for student idealism and protest: from confronting the might of the Soviet Union in Prague to anti-Vietnam war demonstrations in Berkeley. And in 1971, India won its first-ever cricket Test, and the series itself, in the West Indies; the team repeated the feat in England just months later. You could make a persuasive case that there was a change in the country's sense of itself at the time. Triumph in cricket, followed by triumph in war: it was a momentous time. Sure, there would be profound disillusionment with Indira and the experience of the Emergency, but that was still half-a-decade in the future. Until then, the late 1960s and early 1970s – Sen's years at CMC – renewed India's purpose and direction. This was an India pregnant with possibility and promise.

To study at one of the country's finest medical colleges in those years, to learn medicine with CMC's particular emphases, was to be surrounded by that promise.

3

Rural Hospital

One June morning, I walked through the corridors of the Shaheed Hospital in Dalli-Rajhara, Chhattisgarh. I have been in overcrowded hospitals before, but even so, this one was an eye-opener. Narrow to begin with, the corridors were lined on both sides with patients lying on narrow mattresses. Several were asleep, others lying awake or sitting up, rousing themselves for the day. Some had relatives with them. Some had tall metal stands beside them, two plastic drip bottles hanging from the arm on top and trailing down to different patients. Sometimes I saw a patient walking about, carrying his stand. What happened to the other patient's drip, I wondered. I had my answer when a young man walked into the sonography room carrying his bottle. His neighbour in the corridor must have gone walking with the stand.

Beside the stairs on the second floor, a young woman ran past me, sobbing softly. She had burn marks on her jaw, neck and shoulders, and a few open wounds, none of which hid the simple beauty of her face. She had only the *pallu* of her sari to cover herself, but it wasn't wide enough to hide her bare shoulders and the upper part of her chest – bare, because any tighter-fitting clothes, like a blouse, would have been hard on her burned skin. Her mouth was twisted into a sad grimace, and she stopped in front of a bearded young man, imploring him to call the doctor. 'Finish it today!' she pleaded, whimpering, sitting down and repeating her entreaty, there in the middle of a dozen other patients.

He consoled her. 'I'll do it, I'll do it,' he said, gently and patiently. Their two sons arrived, cheery and oblivious to their mother's discomfort. He turned to me, standing there. 'It was an accident, about a month ago,' he said. 'One of the boys ran up behind her when she was cooking and pushed her, and she fell onto the stove.'

'She's better now,' he added quickly, almost as if to reassure me. She had been pleading with him to arrange an 'operation' that day in which, he explained, the doctors would stick some flesh – he used the Hindi word, *maas* – on her left arm. I understood this to be the description of a skin graft. Only then did I notice that the woman's *pallu* covered the burned arm as well; she was as shy of letting others see it as she was about her breasts.

'What do you do?', I asked the man.

'I help at a 'ho-tull' in town,' he said, the word that really means a restaurant.

'What do you there, do you cook?'

'No, I clean tables and vessels.'

'And may I ask, what do they pay you for that?'

'Oh, some seventy-eighty rupees a day.'

'And how much will your hospital bill come to?'

'About the operation, I don't know yet. But this month I've already spent about six thousand rupees here.'

'How did you pay?'

'My seth at the hotel lent me two thousand. My mother gave one thousand. The rest, I'm getting ... *idhar-udhar se*, and I had some money too.'

I stood for a few minutes longer, chatting idly with the man, saying hello to their boys. She sat there. Something buzzed at the back of my mind ... but what?

Now this was an accident. Not a very serious one either: except along her left cheek, her face was untouched. She'd have scars there, on the side of her neck, on her shoulders and perhaps on that arm, but even those would be more in the nature of reminders of how much worse things might have been. Her medical chart said she had suffered 45 per cent burns: bad, but not the end of the world. Why then was she whimpering?

Maybe she was in pain, maybe she was tired of waiting and just wanted the operation over and done with. Or was it the money? While this was not a particularly well-off family, they were not desperately poor either. They would have a debt of 2000 rupees to pay to the hotel owner once the wife went home, but the husband did not seem troubled about that. It did not seem an amount they would struggle haplessly, and for years, to repay.

Then I remembered. Some years ago, I had visited the

family of a farmer in Vidarbha who had killed himself over a debt, leaving behind a distraught wife and two young daughters. That debt, too, was 2000 rupees. The dismal coincidence of the numbers was what had struck me.

Still, as cases go, this was not a particularly unusual one at the Shaheed Hospital, or indeed at other hospitals like it. The hospital was famously built by mineworkers who were tired of unfulfilled promises from mining companies. It perches on a slope at one end of Dalli, overlooking a shallow valley. Across the valley is a taller hill that, at first glance, seems curiously striated. Years of mining have produced the impression of layers.

One day during my visit, I went across the valley to the mines. The scale of the operation was fantastic. At one spot, we looked over the lip of an enormous layered bowl, at the bottom of which we could discern a few trucks and earth movers, beetle-like from this distance. I counted twenty-six separate layers to the bottom, each created as the mines were dug deeper into the earth.

Shaheed Hospital began operations in 1981; one of its early recruits was Binayak Sen, who joined about ten years after graduating from CMC and spent over four years here. Dr Saibal Jana, a small-framed, mild-mannered man now in his mid-fifties, joined at the same time and has become the medical face of the hospital; he is its seniormost and longest-serving doctor.

I wanted to spend time watching Jana at work, watching the hospital function. I wanted to understand what motivates men like him and Sen. I have been in plenty of hospitals –

by middle-age, who hasn't? – but there is still something different about hospitals like Shaheed. Something about the constant crush of patients, overworked doctors, the kinds of complaints, the pressures on doctors' families – and through it all, the commitment to the work.

This is why I sat in Jana's OPD room on the evening I met the woman who had been burned, watching him at work. On average, about 250 patients a day come to the OPD, many from several dozen kilometres away. It was clear, they were not as poor as patients I had seen in other rural hospitals, in Chhattisgarh and elsewhere. Was that a legacy of years of union activity, because of which most people in the area earned a reasonable salary?

The evening OPD sessions were usually less full than in the mornings. The days I visited, it was usually just Jana in the OPD, and the work tired him. He got home well past 8.30 each evening, even though the OPD clinic officially closed at 7.30. Even after that, the nurses on duty often called him in for some emergency or the other. The pressure on him and his family is unmistakable and intense.

The evening I sat in the OPD, this was how one forty-five-minute span went:

A man and his son brought in the younger son, who had suffered an injury under and behind his right ear. It happened when he was bumped about in a bullock cart. The boy was not crying, but looked morose and weary. Jana removed the bandage, moved his head around and felt his jaw. A village doctor had prescribed Cefix, an oral suspension of the antibiotic cefixime, for the boy. Jana told them he only needed to take paracetamol; there was no need to take Cefix. A little puzzled by this advice, a little relieved too, the three got up and left. Jana turned to me and said, 'They do that here,' meaning the doctors who routinely prescribe antibiotics.

An old couple walked in slowly, the man supporting the woman. Her face was twisted in an indescribably strange way, the planes of her jaws at an unfamiliar angle. But that was not her complaint. The man took off her *pallu* and pointed to her sternum. There was a dark brown scar there, almost as if someone had pulled parts of her skin together and tied them into a knot. Jana touched it and said, 'It's a keloid,' which is an excessive growth of scar tissue at the site of a wound. What kind of wound, I wondered fleetingly, did she suffer on her sternum? Jana asked her to get her urine and blood tested, and depending on the results, she might need an injection. He told the couple to get it done that evening, while the hospital technicians were still at work. 'But if we do this now, we won't get transport to go home!' exclaimed the husband. Jana repeated, firmly, that they should get the tests done right then. 'Do it quickly, you will be ok and you'll get your bus.'

The next patient was a ten-year-old boy wearing a checked dhoti, accompanied by his mother. Shyly, he unwrapped the dhoti and I saw a bandage around his penis. Trying to respect his privacy, I turned away and waited for Jana to finish with him.

This is when I noticed that I was drenched in sweat, even though a fan whirled at top speed right above where I was sitting. It was blazing hot outside. Under this high ceiling, surrounded by these whitewashed walls, I remembered school science lessons about air that heats up, collects at the top of a room, and is then blown straight down by a fan. No wonder I was sweating, as was Dr Jana. Also, this must be why the waiting hall outside had a false ceiling made of thatch and was noticeably cooler. The hot air must stay trapped above the panels of thatch.

After the boy came a handsome woman wearing a dull orange sari, her *pallu* draped over her head. She had a soft bump on her head, about the size of a rupee coin. Jana reached out and examined it with his thumb, slightly disturbing the line of *sindoor* in her hair, and told me, 'I can't tell if it is connected to the bone.' Her husband produced a couple of X-rays of her skull. 'Nothing on the X-ray', said Jana. He thought it might be a dermoid cyst, a new phrase to me. 'It's usually benign. If it is not connected to the bone, it can be removed.' He recommended a CT scan. 'How much will it cost?' asked the husband, looking dismayed when Jana said it would be about Rs 2500 or 3000.

The boy who entered next had his left arm in a cast, and wore his shirt so only the right sleeve was filled. There were bruises on his nose, jaw and chin. He must have been in some kind of accident. His X-ray showed the arm bones at a bizarre angle to each other. 'Will it mend on its own?' I asked. Jana nodded: 'Just a matter of time.'

There was a gap before the next patient. Jana told me that in the early days of the hospital, more doctors used to work in the OPD clinics, and there were enough that they could split the incoming patients by complaint and doctors' expertise. But things had changed in a quarter-century. Getting doctors, and especially younger ones, to work here was increasingly difficult. This is a problem common to the other rural health institutions I've visited or know about. And when they find recruits, they don't work regular hours.

Jana and I kept returning to this conversation in my time at the Shaheed Hospital. Walking with him on his rounds the next day, he told me that the hospital needs doctors who will 'give time, think of the patients'. In the early days, doctors had what he called a 'political mindset', both by temperament and as a result of their training. What he meant was that many doctors in those days saw this as a calling: to work among the poor, in urban slums, in rural hinterlands. They developed an 'emotional attachment' to the cause of hospitals like Shaheed, to their unique circumstances and their place in the community.

Before they built the Shaheed Hospital, miners in this area had no access to medical facilities of any kind. They built it without even knowing if there would be doctors willing to work here. As it turned out, Sen and Jana were willing and joined the hospital. It was by no means financial opportunity that attracted them. Instead it was the work, the conditions, the chance to build something to last. Things have changed in a quarter century, for sure. Motivations have. But in the early days, it was also an appreciation for the situation of the miners, of their determination to better their lives on their own, that mattered to doctors like Jana and Sen.

This is the same thought that I had in Vellore. As I understand it, this is where the phrase 'community health' comes from. It means health care must necessarily take into account, and is even a reflection of, the community it serves.

Today, says Jana, again echoing my Vellore thoughts, the mindset of graduating young doctors – perhaps of the country itself – has changed. For example, they rarely work in slums as part of their training. They are interested in and motivated by the chance to make money. They come to Shaheed for two or three years at the most, then move on. Work like this is rarely a career option any more; it is a merely temporary halt on the route to a glitzier somewhere else.

It's not that there are no good doctors graduating from our colleges, says Jana. On the contrary, they are efficient, they are good at their work and are trained in the latest technologies. That applies to his team at Shaheed as well. But in general, today's doctors don't have the same emotional attachment, the kind of orientation or even the sense of mission that an earlier generation did. There must be some who do, of course, but they are not easily found. The result is a looming crisis for places such as this. What happens when doctors like Jana, now middle-aged, retire? Where are the younger doctors, fired with the same purpose and desire that Jana's generation had, twenty-five years ago?

Back in the OPD, someone called Jana out to the hall. I looked around the whitewashed room. There was a chart listing the normal values of various blood metrics: HB, TC, DC, ESR, sugar, urea and creatinin. Another sheet of paper had several instructions, in Hindi, about physiotherapy. Behind me was an examination bed, under which lay several large plastic boxes filled with drugs. On the desk were two stethoscopes, an ophthalmoscope, a TV remote, medical trays, tongue suppressors, a blood pressure instrument and a copy of the *Journal of Dermatological Treatment*, besides assorted inkpads and staplers and pens.

Just an ordinary desk in an ordinary OPD room, its doctor tending to what must be a relatively routine set of OPD patients. And yet Jana had known several of the patients today, often asking them about their circumstances and earlier complaints before they could tell him.

When Jana came back in, a young woman in a green sari with a nose ring was right behind him. She complained of something and he examined her, but she was not really the patient. A minute after her, her mother entered, wearing an olive-green sari and weeping steadily. She wept as Jana greeted her, wept as he checked her blood pressure, wept as he listened to her heart and looked into her throat. It wasn't that there was anything seriously the matter with her, but: 'Please speak to her,' said the daughter. 'The whole day she cries, and she doesn't eat anything.' The mother tried to fall at Jana's feet. He lifted her up, saying, 'You must eat.'

'Her husband died a month ago,' Jana said to me after mother and daughter had left. 'He was a heart patient.' Out of the blue, I remembered an *Outlook* article I had just read about a rural health clinic in Ganiyari, a few hours' journey from Dalli if you take the recently-completed rail link. The report ended with these words: '[O]ver 300 of their patients ... suffer from life-sapping rheumatic heart disease – for [which] there is no affordable surgery available in Chhattisgarh.'[2]

As Jana and I walked back after he had tended to the last OPD patient, I reflected again: the patients and their cases I had encountered that day were not significantly different from others I had seen at other hospitals. But my time in Shaheed served to flesh out a few more details of a picture that, nevertheless, always remains incomplete: what constitutes rural health care in this country.

'The biggest problem that I have encountered in my field experiences', wrote a member of the Planning Commission after visiting Ganiyari in 2007, 'is the unavailability of human resources in health.'[3] She was right: most parts of rural India still struggle to attract and retain doctors and trained nurses. They also suffer from shabbily run Primary Health Centres (PHCs) and poor availability of drugs. All part of that picture I mentioned.

Yet it goes beyond. There's poverty, debt, hunger, unemployment and overcrowding in hospitals; overworked doctors suffer fatigue and stress. There's the distance that patients must travel, sometimes burdened by the lack of public transport.

Cast the net wider still. There's displacement, illiteracy, ignorance, injustice, apathy in government circles, police high-handedness and sometimes, even brutality. In a whole swathe of the country, there's the fear and uncertainty brought about by the presence of Maoists.

To an extent, all these factors play a part in the state of health care, especially in rural areas. They may not all be apparent on a first visit to a place like Dalli-Rajhara and the Shaheed Hospital. But over many visits to many such places over many years, they start to make sense and fit in, like a jigsaw puzzle does.

You see what effect debt, for example, has on a person's health. When you meet a family that has travelled most of a day, changing buses and tempos along the way, to bring a pregnant daughter with a prolapsed uterus to a hospital, you know what impact transport difficulties have on health. When you meet people carrying prescriptions for expensive and yet unnecessary drugs, you understand the need for doctors who are sensitive to the situation of their patients.

You find government charts that are used to track the growth of mineworkers' children. You notice that they come *preprinted* with four 'malnutrition curves', and find that most children are near the worst of those curves. You understand that it makes no sense to use such charts and curves for middle-class urban Indian children, because their weight and height measurements would place them off those charts. Faced with all that, you get an idea of what malnutrition means to many Indians.

When you see a successful rural health clinic that was set up by a team of admittedly idealistic thirty-something doctors fifteen years ago, and note that in all those years they have not been able to attract similarly inclined younger doctors to come work there, and note too that they are reaching fifty and despite their best efforts don't have the energy of those early years – you wonder what the future of the clinic might be. You wonder too why health care for some people is dependent on individual doctors or clinics, rather than be part of a system that functions on its own. You also wonder why those 'some people' I mention are invariably the poorer among us.

To anyone who has spent any time visiting *anganwadis* and clinics in rural India, let alone working there, the situations I've alluded to above will be familiar. Doctors who work in rural health, especially over several years, inevitably begin to understand the deep connections between the conditions they see around them and the health of the people they see every day.

And what is health care without those connections?

My visits to CMC and the Shaheed Hospital leave my mind swirling with questions and thoughts, and I spent a total of a few days at both. Sen spent years at each place. What questions did he have? As Minnie Vaid asks in her book about Sen: 'How could Binayak *not* have been touched by the atmosphere around him?'[4]

4

Interlude: About Two Girls

On the day in December 2010 that Binayak Sen was sentenced to life in prison, I was at a children's court in Mankhurd, an eastern suburb of Bombay.

I was there because I had just been introduced to a young father from Chhattisgarh and his two daughters, aged eight and five respectively. A few nights earlier, a couple I know well had met them on a dusty railway platform in Bilaspur, Chhattisgarh, as they all waited through the gathering dusk for the train to Bombay. They got talking to him, and he said he was taking the girls to Bombay to turn them over to a 'madam'. She had promised him one lakh rupees for them. The money was an attraction, but he wanted to go through with this for these reasons as well:

- His wife abandoned him and the girls three years ago.
- He had a job as a security guard in a Bombay suburb.

He lived in a shed there with twelve other men. This shed was no place for two young girls to also live.

- There had already been times when some men in the shed tried to do 'dirty things' with his girls.
- He had no way to ensure the safety of the girls.
- Better, all things considered, to sell them to a madam.

Aghast to hear his story, the couple asked him not to act in haste and assured him that once in Bombay, they would try to help. When they reached, they got in touch with a shelter for street children in Andheri. The person in charge was willing to take the girls in, but said they would need a court order before he could do so. That was when the couple asked me to drive them all to the Mankhurd court.

Sometime that afternoon, as we waited to speak to the judge, my phone beeped. It was a text message announcing the verdict in Binayak Sen's case. It beeped again after a while. This time, it announced Sen's life sentence.

Why, apart from it happening on the day of his sentence, is this story relevant to Binayak Sen?

Because this young father and his girls offer a glimpse of the way a lot of Indians live. If I want to consider the meaning of Sen's case, such glimpses are inescapable.

But consider first the reactions to Sen's conviction that day. Many Indians were appalled, above all because we could see no evidence for the charges against him. That a state's judicial machinery could ask for and obtain a conviction – a life sentence at that – on such grounds should alarm us all.

But many other Indians felt quite different emotions. 'An antinational got what he deserved', said a typical message that also beeped into my phone that same afternoon. For such people, the only thing that mattered was that Sen was accused of meeting an imprisoned sixty-seven-year-old man the state machinery called a Maoist. This meeting, no questions asked, was enough to call Sen an 'antinational'. One mention of the word 'Maoist', and plenty of people otherwise skeptical of governments become instant believers.

On this day that Sen was sentenced to life in prison, I heard a judge in Mankhurd tell a father who feared for his daughters' safety: 'You should have made a police complaint about the men who tried to mess with your daughter!'

'I tried', said the father. 'They told me to go away.'

'You should have gone back, ten times if necessary!' said the judge. 'This is a question of their moral security!' But this judge who was concerned about moral security refused to let the man take his daughters to the shelter that was willing to take them in. Not even for the night.

'Go back to where you live,' said the judge. 'Make a police complaint about the men first, then approach the children's court.'

That was the end of that. These were the lessons I learned that day:

- A young man can find no worthwhile work in his home in Chhattisgarh.
- He comes to the big city and makes Rs 3500 a month, far more than he would at home.
- Back in his village, his wife runs away, abandoning their daughters.

- Left with no choice, he brings his daughters to the big city to live with him.
- Grown men do 'dirty' things with the little girls.
- He decides to sell them to a 'madam' for a lakh of rupees, which tempts him because it's nearly two-and-a-half years' salary.
- When he's persuaded via a chance encounter to try a saner route instead, a judge tells him to take them back to the same place where depraved grown men live.

Poverty and deprivation in India have plenty of dimensions: hard lives, injustice, non-existent health care, apathetic authorities and more. I could list figures and cite examples. This experience in court was one. This is the context for the rise of Maoists and the reason they have such a lot of support in areas like Chhattisgarh.

Back in Mankhurd: After the futile court appearance, the couple suggested to the father that they would help him find a hostel for his girls in Chhattisgarh, a place where they would be safe while he returned to work in Bombay. He made up his mind. They would spend the night on the platform and catch the next morning's Gitanjali Express back to Bilaspur.

We sat with them for a dinner of *dal-chawal* and scrambled eggs before they left.

'Eat properly,' he said to one daughter when she didn't want any more to eat. 'There's no food for two days now.'

Context. It's everything.

5

Man of the 21st

On 18 April 2011, Binayak Sen walked out of Raipur jail, free on bail that the Supreme Court had granted him three days earlier. There was a crush of journalists outside, later a press conference in the compound of the block of flats where he lives in Raipur, and innumerable appearances on TV.

Over the next few days, I watched the coverage and read about him in the newspapers. Through it all, I was struck by some of the things Sen said. Here was a man who had been sentenced to spend the rest of his life in prison and had already spent nearly two-and-a-half years there. He had become the focus of a worldwide campaign which followed his trial to secure his release. He had also stimulated debates on the meaning of sedition, how to face the spectre of Naxalites and the constitutionality and morality of citizen militias like Salwa Judum. You would expect him to talk about such issues when he was released on bail. And he did. But reluctantly. He seemed far more interested in talking about something that had to do only peripherally with his prison stay.

Here, for example, are some lines from an interview he gave to Aman Sethi of the *Hindu*:[5]

> At present, the greatest violence is structural violence. Violence is not restricted to a few groups; it pervades the structure of our society. We need to break out of this structure of violence through a process of dialogue.
>
> Q: Could you elaborate on this idea of structural violence?
>
> By structural violence I refer to the fact that half our children and our adults in this country suffer from malnutrition. Malnutrition casts a dark shadow over other diseases like malaria and tuberculosis.
>
> For example, a study by the National Nutrition Monitoring Bureau says that more than 60 per cent of Scheduled Tribes have a body mass index (BMI) of less than 18.5. According to the World Health Organisation, if more than 40 per cent of the population of a community has a BMI of less than 18.5, the community can be considered to be in a condition of famine. A third of our live births have low birth weights, this is what I mean when I talk of structural violence.

It says something about Sen's way of thinking that what

he wanted to talk about, on being released from prison, was malnutrition, BMI, low birthweights and structural violence. Through his personal nightmare and the implications it would have for the rest of his life, through the relief that must have washed over him at the time – through all that, Sen wanted the focus to remain on malnutrition.

Yet this is only logical, natural, if you start digging into the case. For your reasoning might follow a line that goes something like this:

Why was Sen really arrested? Perhaps the government of Chhattisgarh thought he was helping Naxalites? Perhaps they were not pleased by his criticism of Salwa Judum?

And what is Salwa Judum? In 2006, what some describe as a people's movement arose in Chhattisgarh to resist the Naxalites. (In an August 2010 affidavit to the Supreme Court, the Chhattisgarh government called it a 'spontaneous peaceful people's uprising against Naxalite violence.'[6]) This was *Salwa Judum*, a tribal language phrase that has been translated as, among other things, 'Purification Hunt'.

It soon found intangible and tangible support from across the Chhattisgarh political spectrum. The government trained young men to join the movement, calling them 'Special Police Officers' or SPOs, giving them arms and an honorarium of Rs 3000 a month.

Salwa Judum was controversial from the start. Its cheerleaders applauded because the Judum attacked Naxalites, eye for an eye. Its critics, Sen among them, counted its atrocities, decrying the use of otherwise untrained young civilians on the frontlines of what was essentially a war.

In 2011, the Supreme Court declared groups like the Salwa Judum illegal and unconstitutional. It directed the government of Chhattisgarh to stop their operations and 'recall all firearms issued to any of the SPOs, whether current or former.'[7]

Unconstitutionality aside, even after five years of Salwa Judum operations, Naxalites remain active. Why, and why are they so hard to defeat? Not easy to answer briefly, but at least part of the reason lies in things that blight a lot of Indian lives – poor health care, injustice, non-existent education facilities, malnutrition and more. The dissatisfaction this results in finds an outlet in protest against the state.

Thus the link to malnutrition.

The message, then, must be this: when you want to fight Naxalites, Salwa Judum gets you nowhere. Start instead with the challenge of tackling malnutrition. Recognize that it exists, find ways to address it. We may never end it altogether, but addressing it gives people one less reason to turn to the empty promise of Naxalites. This fights Naxalites in the most effective way: by undermining them.

This was what Sen had on his mind, when he walked free on bail. The focus on malnutrition, even at such a time, is no surprise. He has consistently spoken of concerns like these, going back to his days at CMC. You might see this as a commentary on the man, but on his country as well.

Sen has a deliberate, measured way of speaking, whether in a speech or in conversation. You get the impression he thinks through every word he says. If you ask him a question, he invariably takes a few seconds to put together a carefully thought-out answer. What he says is rarely casual, never off-the-cuff. There is a seriousness to the man that, in turn, makes demands of the listener: that you pay attention and think about what he is saying. You see the same sense of gravity if you watch his television interviews. But the more interesting thing is, it seems to rub off on his interviewers.

I remember a television interview right after his release in April 2011. The NDTV anchor Vikram Chandra kept referring to Sen as 'sir'. I don't watch TV enough to know if that is Chandra's preferred appellation for male guests, but I wonder if he has ever addressed other men sentenced to life imprisonment as 'sir'. Yet most people use that term for Sen naturally.

Like in August 2011, when Sen spoke at a Rotary meeting in Bombay, and nearly everyone there called him 'sir' too. It was refreshing, then, to hear Sen say to Dolly Thakore, the ex-TV anchor and actress, his host that afternoon: 'Please don't call me sir, just use Binayak! After all, I'm a big fan of yours, I watched you on stage in Calcutta years ago!'

This informality better fits the impression I've gathered from people who know Sen well. They don't speak of gravity and seriousness, but of a genial man who likes music and singing in his deep voice. One has often told me of Sen's fondness for old jazz standards, as well as for singers of the '60s and '70s such as Paul Anka and Engelbert Humperdinck. Another mutual friend spoke of his hearty laugh, and the jokes he likes to tell. I haven't heard the singing voice, nor yet seen Sen sway to Anka and Humperdinck. But I have heard that laugh. It is an open and fully felt thing.

I once spent an evening with Sen and a few friends in the Bombay suburb of Bandra. He was visibly tired from a long day of speeches, meetings and travel across the city. Still, he chatted softly with nearly everyone present, one-on-one rather than participating in the larger conversation. Food arrived from a nearby kabab restaurant. There was not enough for everyone present, so Sen searched for a knife in the kitchen, sliced his kathi roll firmly and precisely down the middle and shared it with me.

The friends were chirpy, full of fun and energy. One recited long Hindi poems he had composed. Another wanted to record Sen appealing for signatures for a petition to repeal the law of sedition. It would carry weight if made by Sen, a man trying to fight off a charge of exactly that offence. When it was time to record, Sen was no longer his informal but weary self. After a few seconds to think and compose himself, he was back to the measured cadences, the more formal words that typify his public speaking, focusing fully and earnestly on the issue.

The clip is on YouTube. Watching it later, I suddenly thought of a secret nobody else knows: he had just wolfed down his half of a kathi roll.

Is Sen's seriousness, his earnestness, a result of his time in prison? The answer to that is that his earliest writings reflect the same focus, the desire to examine an issue for broader causes and implications.

For example: working at CMC, Vellore, in 1975, the 24 year-old Sen entered an essay competition whose theme was: 'The present system of medical education in the country is said to have an elitist orientation with an urban bias. Please suggest a medical education for undergraduates which can effectively cater to the needs of the vast majority of the population in the country.' Sen's essay, 'A Suggested System of Undergraduate Medical Education', won him first prize.

Some excerpts from the essay[8]:

> [Many doctors from] the All India Institute of Medical Sciences [AIIMS] are stationed outside their country. The situation at my alma mater, the Christian Medical College, Vellore, is not much better. Both these institutions regard themselves, and are regarded by others, as among the foremost medical colleges in India. If the graduates of some of the other colleges have not left, it is not for want of trying. In a milieu where international fame rather than local effectiveness is the determinant of success, professors with foreign contacts congregate in the big name colleges ...
>
> Academic success is not the sole determinant of success as a physician: attitudes, values and motives are equally important. The successful doctor in any field must have, in addition to good physical and mental health, certain personality traits ...
>
> Anyone seriously interested in making the services of medical graduates available to people in the rural areas

would realize that the most ordinary candidate willing and eager to serve the rural populace is more suited to his purpose than the most brilliant candidate with his hopes set abroad ...

It is assumed that somehow, when the student emerges from in between the portals of his alma mater, he will automatically acquire the totally unfamiliar motivation, orientation, skills and knowledge necessary to enable him to function effectively in a rural setting. Not unexpectedly, this does not happen.

Reading these paragraphs over thirty-five years later, you can imagine them being written today, which is both a reflection of the way Sen thought about the issue then, and a sign of how little has changed in the way doctors are trained now. For me, the phrase that jumps out above is 'local effectiveness'. Concerned with the famous 'brain drain' at the time, Sen makes clear the distinction between the desire to go abroad, on one hand, and this local effectiveness on the other. There's a summation of what we must value in our doctors: not that they find fame and money, but that they are effective in their work. An Indian medical education must not just teach doctors about rural health care, it must also make students see it as a worthwhile career choice.

But if the brain drain weighed on his mind in 1975, over the years Sen has focused more on the meaning and imperative of rural health care within India. Some of these imperatives find mention at various points in this book. In essence, I'm alluding to the realization that health care is about much more than just clinical or medical issues. Sen's thinking and writing spelled out that realization in various ways.

In 1999, Sen wrote an essay for *Medico Friend Circle Bulletin*, titled 'People's Health Care Initiatives in Chhattisgarh'. Here are a few lines from that piece[9]:

> Since many of the activities that could be classified under preventive ... health care (such as the struggle for safe drinking water, the campaign against liquor sales and alcohol abuse) were being directly undertaken by the [Shaheed Hospital in Dalli-Rajhara], my medical colleagues and I were able to concentrate on building up a culturally acceptable alternative paradigm of clinical care:
>
> 1. An overall emphasis on rational practices in health care ...
> 2. Demystification of technology ...
> 3. Constant attempts to minimize the distinction between mental and manual labour.
> 4. Democratization of all decision-making processes.
>
> We tried in Shaheed Hospital to incorporate a model of science in which manual and mental skills were given equal importance, and in which the entire range of workers were able to participate.

What intrigues me here is the range of issues that Sen describes as health care initiatives. First is the subtle mention that 'the struggle for safe drinking water' and fighting 'alcohol abuse' are part of preventive health care. Then he underlines broader themes that shrink the gap between patient and physician. There is the emphasis on the dignity of labour, not just in treating mental and manual skills the same, but as vital to a hospital's functioning. And for anyone who has spent time in an Indian hospital, the idea of demystifying technology will resonate.

The wider implications of health care remained a concern for Sen. In 2004, CMC honoured him with its annual Paul Harrison Award for Meritorious Service in Rural Areas. In his acceptance speech, Sen spoke again about these wider implications, hinting inadvertently at themes that would, three years later, overtake his life. He said[10]:

> The first point that I would like to make is about the primacy of politics in any relevant programme for health and health care. By politics I do not mean the farcical electoral charades of political parties, but the matrix of power that determines control over resources at every level of community.

Elaborating on this idea, Sen narrated a story from Chhattisgarh. During a famine there, 10,000 tonnes of grain lay in a particular Food Corporation of India (FCI) godown. Yet its manager told Sen that even though he fed the Public Distribution System (PDS) from his stocks, 'there was no one to buy it'.

Why?

Plenty of people had BPL ('Below Poverty Line') ration cards, which entitled them to subsidized grain prices. Yet they could not afford even the lowered prices. But it's worse than that. 'The BPL identification process,' he said, 'itself is another scandal.' Governments are reluctant to recognize as poor all those who cannot get enough to feed themselves every day. So plenty of poor Indians cannot get BPL cards.

'I hope I have made it clear,' Sen said, 'that politics – politics in its broadest sense – is a highly contingent factor where health is concerned.'

From worrying about the brain drain, he was now interested in a fleshed-out, more complex vision of healthcare, one that would understand and address all the factors that affect it. And three years later, politics in some sense turned Sen's life inside-out.

Since his release on bail, Sen has spoken often about another kind of connection: between malnutrition and secession. At the Rotary Club meeting in Bombay, he told an audience of doctors, lawyers and businessmen, gathered at the Taj Mahal Hotel, about his belief that there was a 'stable famine' in the country.

What does this mean? Sen explained that the body mass index (BMI), calculated as an individual's weight in kilograms divided by the square of his height in metres, is a 'rapid and robust indicator of nutritional status' in adults. There are better ways to estimate this, of course, but because the BMI is easily calculated, the phrase 'rapid and robust' applies. The normal range of the BMI is considered to be 18.5 to 25.

The same National Nutrition Monitoring Bureau findings Sen mentioned to the *Hindu* show that 37 per cent of India's adult population has a BMI below 18.5. In other words, nearly two of every five Indian adults is undernourished. According to the World Health Organization, he told the assembled Rotarians, any community in which more than 40 per cent of the population is undernourished (with BMIs below 18.5) is said to be suffering a famine. India's adults, therefore, are close to being considered famine-stricken.

Add to this the plight of India's under-five children, 47 per cent of whom are undernourished, and we are drawing perilously close to the 40 per cent famine line. Consider too that the 37 per cent figure masks the condition of smaller groups of Indians – as he pointed out, 50 per cent of our Scheduled Tribes and 60 per cent of the Scheduled Castes have BMIs under 18.5.

This is why Sen spoke, in the Rotary meeting, of a 'stable famine'; this is why he told the *Hindu* that we are 'walking in a state of famine'. In fact, Sen even suggested that this situation fits the definition of genocide: not by guns or machetes or gas chambers, but by creating conditions for communities 'in which the survival of [these communities] is put at risk'. Such conditions hold even though India actually produces enough food to feed all Indians. Only, it doesn't reach all Indians.

'Please examine,' said Sen, 'the moral hazard of the situation in which we are placed today.' For Sen, the stable famine he mentions is 'anterior to the whole argument about sedition'.

At one level, some might see this as suggesting that things like sedition and free speech are possibly esoteric, somewhat remote concerns for people fighting the elemental battles of malnourishment and famine. Yet it is hardly my intention, and certainly not Sen's, to brush aside those who value free speech. The point he made that day is that in his experience, for people suffering through this state of perpetual stable famine, what's at stake is survival itself:

> Our experience with organisations working among tribal people and the experience of others working in rural and urban settings shows that these communities have survived because of their access to common property resources (such as water, land, forests and knowledge of biodiversity).[11]

Yet after twenty years of globalization and liberalization, these communities' access to such common property resources is being eroded and blocked – in Sen's words, 'expropriated' – by the State itself.

That is the context 'in which we have to consider the crime of sedition'.

'How you respond to the charge of sedition?', NDTV's Vikram Chandra asked Sen. 'Do you think at any time in any way you've been disloyal to this nation?'

Sen replied:

> More important than what I feel is what the Supreme Court says, that there's no evidence of any seditious activity against me. But the point is that there are thousands of other people who are in a similar situation. And I have never had any feeling of disloyalty for the

people of this country. I'm proud to be an Indian, and I'm proud to be part of the Indian people.[12]

The issue is not about charging Sen himself with sedition. Instead, it is that whoever protests such processes is accused of the crime. Section 124 of the IPC – the section dealing with sedition – and other laws are being used 'to suppress dissent and resistance to expropriation across our land.' Thousands of Indians are in jail, charged with such crimes. 'They are in a hopeless situation', Sen said, because they haven't got anything like the attention that Sen himself has got.

There's little doubt that the policies of the Indian government make life itself harder for a lot of its citizens.

The question is this: are we willing to see the rise of the Maoist movement in this light? Leave aside the violence of the Maoists for a minute. Are we willing to concede that there's a legitimate dissatisfaction and frustration a lot of Indians feel, and that Maoists have tapped into and built on it? That this dissatisfaction has to do with fundamental worries about survival itself, such as famine and undernourishment? That this frustration, left to fester, will inevitably lead to protest? And if we are willing to concede this much, is charging such people with committing crimes, including sedition, a reasonable way to address these worries?

'I hope I have been able to convince you,' Sen told his Rotary audience, 'that issues related to human rights are of central importance to the practice of health care.'

Yet again, the same equation, the same understanding of broader themes that have a bearing on health care. When you practice medicine, especially in rural India, you cannot help but run up against a number of these issues. If you react to them as any reasonably aware and thinking human being would, should you be charged with sedition?

Sen's thinking, his speeches, the case itself, pose this question above all, for us to answer.

In what people say about Sen, there's an articulation of the same concern with human rights – indeed, with the human *condition* – that Sen speaks about. This always reminds me of an article from another context in the *New York Times*.[13] During a 2011 protest against cuts in US government programmes for the poor and hungry, the journalist Mark Bittman met David Beckmann, a priest participating in the protest. 'You can't have real religion,' Beckmann told Bittman, 'unless you work for justice for hungry and poor people.' Bittman comments: 'I don't think you can have much humanity, either.'

Profiles of Sen, interviews with him and articles about his case invariably offer glimpses of such themes.

Writing in *Outlook*, for example, Anjali Puri reported that when speaking to her about conditions in jail, Sen said he couldn't 'divorce' them from 'those of other people around me ... How people sleep and eat is not important. The important thing about the people in jail is their condition of hopelessness – because the legal process passes so many of them by.'[14]

Similarly, in an interview with *Frontline,*[15] Justice Rajinder Sachar was asked: 'Why was Binayak Sen picked out and systematically victimized in Chhattisgarh?' He replied:

> We have a strong PUCL[16] unit in the State. It has been functioning for long, and it has also been very critical of the government, especially after Salwa Judum. … Binayak took an active part in the PUCL's opposition to Salwa Judum. Because of his work in the tribal areas, Binayak was coming into contact with tribal people every day.
>
> … The PUCL is against any violence. We don't even support Naxalite violence because it gives the government an opportunity to suppress a genuine people's movement.
>
> … There are so many poor men and women who could be Maoist sympathizers. How can a social worker or an activist not be in touch with them if they are working in that area?

Elsewhere in that same issue of *Frontline,* another article has these lines[17]:

> During the five years he spent in [Dalli-Rajhara, Sen] found extreme levels of poverty and malnutrition in central India and also understood that massive state injustices, such as displacement without rehabilitation of tribal people, played a big role in the prevalence of these conditions in the rural hinterland, home to most of India's mineral and natural resources. He found that

> the forest villages, illegal in the eyes of the state, and the natural resources were the only means of survival for the tribal people. These areas had no schools, no public health centres and no state programmes that their residents could gain access to.
>
> ... With the formation of Chhattisgarh State, he became an active human rights activist, too, as that work related directly to his activities in health care.

In fact, only a few years after Chhattisgarh was formed as a new state in 2000, its government asked Sen to join an advisory committee on health affairs (as you will read later in this book).

What then happened to make the government turn against him so completely, to the extent that they arrested him and sought life imprisonment for him in court? Based on his experience in public health, Sen could not help asking questions about rights violations. In turn, this only annoyed the authorities in Chhattisgarh. Yet, as the *Frontline* report tells us: 'there is nothing he has done that human rights advocates across the world have not done.'

The link, again, between health and human rights.

A report in *Tehelka* describes a court appearance by Sen in February 2008. Nothing much happened that day. When the police returned him to their van to transport him back to prison, Sen 'presses his face against the iron bars and says [something] urgently' to the assembled press. What did he say, that day after a court hearing? Something about his case? The injustice of it? The conditions in jail? What?

This:

> You must understand, there is a Malthusian process of exclusion going on in the country. You cannot create two categories of human beings. Everybody must wake up to this, otherwise soon it will be too late. ... I have never condoned Maoist violence. It is an invalid and unsustainable movement. Along with the Salwa Judum, it has created a dangerous split in the tribal community. But the grievances are real. ... You cannot create two categories of people.[18]

Such are the thoughts of this man on trial for his life.

As a curious postscript, the same *Tehelka* article reports a question asked by Vishwa Ranjan, the Director General of Police, Chhattisgarh. Speaking of Sen, he asks: 'Why does he criticize the Salwa Judum more than the Maoists?'

As if criticism can or should be measured. As if a man's guilt depends on who or what he criticizes, and how much.

Such are the thoughts, in contrast, of a man charged with upholding the law.

I first met Binayak Sen in early May 2011, a couple of weeks after the Supreme Court granted him bail and he was released from jail in Raipur. It was before nine in the morning when I arrived at the Sens' farm on the outskirts of Raipur. A few dogs sniffed curiously at my shins and a small team was working on some repairs on a low building on the premises.

Sen greeted me and we sat chatting on a parapet outside: how was your trip, hope your health is better, and the like. His wife Ilina emerged soon after, with biscuits and tea. After a while, Sen rose and went into the house for something. 'The time in jail has left him a little confused,' said Ilina. 'He's forgotten how to use ATMs, for example.'

When Sen returned, he told me of an incident from the previous day. He was walking the dogs on the road outside the farm, as he did every day. An open jeep passed him, driving fairly fast. It suddenly braked and stopped about 100 metres ahead of Sen. Then it reversed, also at speed, and drew up alongside him. In the jeep was a bearded young man wearing shades. He stared at Sen for a few seconds, then suddenly shifted into gear and roared off.

Nothing overt had happened, yet this odd encounter had clearly shaken him and Ilina. 'We've seen posters in Raipur,' said Ilina, 'posters with Binayak's picture on them, saying 'Traitors must be hanged".

When I was done with my tea, two of the workers came up to discuss some aspect of their repairs. The building was one that the Sens built to use for occasional courses, for example to train health workers. We walked over. It wasn't finished yet, but it gave the impression of light and air. On one side stood a wooden ladder that did not inspire much confidence. One of the men held it firm as Sen and I climbed to the curved roof. It was laid with bits of broken tile, making for a smooth, cool surface to walk on in my bare feet. From below, the man directed us a few steps to our left. Sen pointed out a long crack that ran across the roof. As we walked around the roof, we saw more cracks that needed repair.

Back on terra firma a few minutes later, Sen took me into the house and produced two slices of toast.

It was a morning remarkable only for its ordinariness. It prompted me, later that day, to ask Sen, what was a typical day in jail like?

'I usually woke at 6 a.m.', he said. The warders would open the door of the cell, and Sen would go out for a walk in the courtyard. At about 7, there was tea, and breakfast an hour later. The newspapers of the day, always censored – that is, with jagged holes where material unfit for Sen's eyes had been excised – arrived at about 11. Local papers were available, but Sen had specifically asked for the *Hindu*. Since the *Hindu* does not have an edition printed in Chhattisgarh, he'd get the previous day's Delhi edition, with day-old news.

With holes in it, that is.

He'd read the paper, do some exercise and walk some more. Lunch was served at about noon. In the afternoon, he'd read some more – he had access to a few books, though the prison library 'had no books worth reading'. If there was time, the prisoners would sit around and talk about their cases and the news. There was a TV on which they could watch the news on the government's own Doordarshan channel. In fact, that was how he found out about his own bail. After dinner at about 7 p.m., he would be locked into his cell for the night.

A few physical details rounded out this picture. His cell had no windows, only a grill set in the door. He was allowed visits by family once a month, and he quickly realized how important it was just to be able to touch whoever came to visit. Sometimes prisoners were separated from their families by a double grill and could not touch them. He also spoke about feeding a cat that lived inside the jail, one egg yolk a day.

More ordinariness. If I was expecting stories of shackles and beatings and fights to the death with other prisoners, Sen's account showed only that prison life was so bland that blandness itself was the penalty.

No wonder he seemed confused to his wife. No wonder he had forgotten how to use ATMs.

When I met Ilina Sen a few months earlier, she had spoken at length about the case, particularly various flaws in the prosecution, some of which appear later in this book. This segued almost naturally into a discussion about the connection between health care and other seemingly unrelated issues.

Hunger played a key role in Sen's work, she said. Once, he heard about ration shops in Surguja district in Chhattisgarh. They had food available for sale and people even had ration cards, but they could not afford the prices the shops charged. Thus hunger was widespread, which led to malnutrition, which led to health issues doctors were confronted with.

How does a doctor who works in such areas close his eyes to a clear, direct link like this? How does he work without wondering what it will take for people to at least afford ration shop prices? And yet the evidence is that many doctors don't think about these things. Those who do, said Ilina, are 'anachronisms'.

Sen had always believed in speaking his mind. He was often frankly critical of people, never shying away from hurting sentiments if necessary. He had contempt for friends or colleagues who helped prop up corrupt regimes and spoke publicly about them. He raised questions about Salwa Judum. Yet he did not think of the consequences of speaking so freely. Ilina reflected that her husband knew that government machineries are often corrupt, but he did not understand the lengths to which a state would go to crucify him for speaking his mind.

Back in Raipur, done with the toast and a cup of coffee, I asked Sen: 'What about the case? How do you react to all that it has done to you?'

A short pause while he gathered his thoughts, then a swiftly rendered few sentences in response. From my notes, they went like this:

'I am hopeful,' he began, 'that the verdict, the life sentence, will be overturned. Because there's no logic in it. There's no evidence of any criminal act that I committed. Not even the state has accused me of anything criminal. They have accused me of meeting certain people. But just meeting people is not a crime.' He repeated: 'The state has not accused me of any crime.'

Referring to his colleagues in the PUCL in Chhattisgarh, he went on: 'We're very clear that government policy was behind the rise of the Salwa Judum. We knew we were opposing Salwa Judum, and thus the government, but that's our democratic right. Salwa Judum has caused the burning of houses, raping of women, killing of civilians by armed militias. In opposing all this, in demanding the legitimate rights of people to justice, we were fulfilling the demands of our conscience. This is required of any loyal citizen.'

But it was clear that the state intended to suppress their protest with punitive action. The government was angry with the work of the PUCL, but there was no way they would not continue with it. 'Once we deny civil liberties, we no longer know where we are headed. Democracy and civil liberties must always be maintained and protected. And in fact that in itself is the justification for a concern for civil liberties and human rights: that they contribute to the integrity of a democratic system. When you ignore them, you call that integrity into question.'

All of which sounded reasonable to me. Yet I knew that one of the prime accusations against Sen was that he met a Maoist ideologue, Narayan Sanyal, in jail several times, and carried some letters for him to a man called Piyush Guha. What about meeting Sanyal, I asked Sen. And those letters?

After their first meeting, the jail officer asked Sen to get permission for subsequent visits from the senior superintendent. He got that. But the jail officials were present at every meeting, extra-vigilant in their body-searches before and after. There was a jail register that Sen signed, with every visit.

And yet the government accused him of smuggling letters to Guha, now his fellow-accused. Apart from anything else, the police cannot even prove that Sen and Guha actually met. And in any case, the letters don't contain any seditious material. In fact, there has been little critical evaluation of all the evidence the prosecution produced in pursuing this case. Yet it would be 'retrograde', said Sen, if his release on bail resulted in such an evaluation only for his case. Instead, it should lay down a general principle about the need to carefully examine evidence.

This led Sen to another point about the process of justice. There must be greater public oversight of whatever is happening in our courts. This needs a committed audience, whose critical participation in the process – instead of trying to insulate courts from view – must be welcomed and seen as a step towards a better quality of justice. The aim always should be to have an open court.

He and his PUCL colleagues do not approve of any violence, whether by individuals, the state, or non-state groups like the Maoists. I listened to this, thinking of the number of times Sen has been asked what his connection was to Maoists, whether he approved of the violence they perpetrated, and if so why.[19]

Throughout our conversation, I got the impression that Sen was discussing these details – the conditions he faced in jail, his thoughts on Maoist violence and the case against him – on sufferance. In his mind, the whole case was only incidentally about him. At one point, he made his argument this way: 'Whatever has happened to me is the result of the suffering of thousands of people. Any personal imprint would be 'ghoulish" (he really used that word). He was chafing at the bit to return to discussing the situation of Indians who suffer 'structural violence': the themes of malnutrition, BMI and famine.

But Sen had a broader point to make. The communities that face this structural violence are facing annihilation – strong word, but Sen clearly saw it as possible – because of famine and an inability to survive.

What advice was the Indian state giving them?

To him, it was particularly important for doctors to think about these things. A 2008 report[20] by a committee headed by Sir Michael Marmot, for example, said inequity is killing people on a grand scale around the world. If we were to measure it, India would display some of the highest levels of inequity in the world. Nutrition has 'implicit within it' the idea of inequity. 'If we doctors are not able to address the problem of inequity and chronic undernutrition,' said Sen, 'our duty as physicians is incomplete.'

It took him a long time, he said, to understand this connection. He had teachers who had worked on malnutrition and taught that the primary duty of the doctors they were training was to address the problems of the poor. Sen mentioned the nineteenth-century German pathologist Rudolf Virchow, known for saying 'politics is nothing but medicine writ large.'[21] If people in medicine truly have the interests of their patients in mind, they will have to ask the series of ever-broader questions that come up during their work: from malnutrition to injustice to civil liberties, allowing always for the overlap between themes. And if they are willing to do that, doctors cannot help but bump up against the practice of politics.

'I don't know much about the Maoists,' Sen explained. 'I am not a political person and I never have sought a political identity. I just followed the logic of my profession.' But that logic itself leads a doctor to issues like inequity, and thus to the realm of politics: politics in the sense of how groups of citizens manoeuvre and negotiate their place in society.

These were the serious, if not outright depressing themes we discussed that day on Sen's Raipur farm. And through it all I was conscious that this was a man with a sentence of life imprisonment on his head. Even if Sen seemed a little confused to his wife, he did not come across to me as downcast or pessimistic, in no way weighed down by the years in which his life had been turned upside down.

'I do believe,' he said that first evening, 'that people are interested in peace. The issue of this enormous tension that's at the heart of our society is something that all of us find unsatisfactory. Given a chance to reduce that tension, I believe the majority in this country would be interested. And so dialogue is the road towards peace: dialogue and equity, justice and equity.'

If enough people of goodwill talk to one another, Sen believes, a dialogue will ensue.

Cynical as I am about terms like goodwill and dialogue, I had to ask: are you confident there are 'enough people of goodwill', and that they will really 'talk to each other'? 'What gives you hope about these things?' I asked.

Hope, replied Sen, is a duty enjoined on us by our present situation.

6

The Case

Binayak Sen was arrested in May 2007.

The news reminded me of an argument with a journalist some years earlier. Only days before we met, there had been a large demonstration in Bombay against the war in Iraq. This journalist was asked to cover it. Something about it had irked him no end, and when we met he was still consumed with indignation.

He rattled through some of the usual arguments: why a protest in India about a faraway war that has nothing to do with us? Why the solidarity with foreign Muslims? Weren't these people worried about how evil this Saddam is? Didn't they think he should be stopped?

Then he pulled out his clincher. 'Did you notice,' he asked, wagging a finger in my face, 'that several of these people were carrying portraits of Osama bin Laden?'

For him, this was indecent public behaviour, but also clearly a terrible crime. He wasn't happy when I asked, 'So?'

'What do you mean, so? You can't display a picture of a terrorist! It's illegal! How can you ignore such a thing?'

'Illegal? But what's the crime they committed?' I asked. For to me it was clear, and I was sure I didn't need training in law to know that simply holding up a picture is not (yet) a crime in India. It might be a portrait of the world's most-wanted terrorist, it might offend any number of people, but just carrying it breaks no law.

The journalist looked angrily at me. 'I know they must have broken some law!' he said. 'I'll find out which one and call you tomorrow to tell you!'

Years later, I am still waiting for his call.

Similar thoughts came to me after reading about the case against Binayak Sen. The charge sheet against him claims he committed a number of crimes – claims that deserve examination of course. But the basis of suspicion against him, and thus the original crime he was supposed to have committed, was that he visited an aging Marxist ideologue, Narayan Sanyal, in the Raipur jail. He was also supposed to have carried three letters from Sanyal, thus being a 'courier' for the Maoist movement. His visits were approved by jail authorities every time, and as you will see, the letters are innocuous – but in truth, those caveats are irrelevant.

I say this not because I have trained as a lawyer. No, I'm another ordinary citizen of my country who is baffled even by reading about this case. Am I missing something? Where's the crime? No doubt people were offended by Sen's actions, like the journalist was offended by people who held up bin Laden portraits. Indeed, talking later to his family and friends, I was struck by how many of them told me that they had warned him to be careful, because he was doing things that would annoy a lot of people. Besides, I have lost track of the number of people who have written articles about Sen, or emailed messages to me, expressing outrage that he had these 'contacts' with Maoists and therefore they had grown to 'loathe' him.

But where's the crime? None of the friends and family told me that they thought Sen was breaking the law. None of the articles and email messages spelled out his crime. In merely visiting a prisoner, even a prisoner who is a Maoist, there is no law broken. In merely carrying letters, even letters from a Maoist, there is no law broken. You don't need legal training to know this.

That there are ways to interpret our laws such that someone accused of these things can be charged and punished is a different matter. After all, the idea of a judicial system is predicated on interpreting laws in court and applying them to given situations. This is why justice is a human endeavour, not one entrusted to a machine programmed to apply laws and deliver a verdict.

Look at it this way: killing someone is a crime. Burglary is a crime. Inciting violence is a crime. We know these things without needing to read the Indian Penal Code. In much the same way, we know: not even the IPC makes meeting a prisoner, by itself, a crime. We haven't made carrying notes a crime. We haven't made carrying photographs a crime. I'm alluding here to the spirit of the law, and it is my belief that a reasonably aware citizen is, and must be, imbued with such spirit. It gives us a reliable sense of what's right in India, what's wrong.

It is this spirit that I will both rely on and seek to invoke in this examination of Binayak Sen's case.

Narayan Sanyal, now over seventy-years old, is a prisoner in Raipur's Central Jail. In April 2006, his brother Radhamadhab wrote to the superintendent of the jail, marking a copy to Binayak Sen. In the letter, he said his brother had been medically examined and needed surgery for what he described as 'Palmer's contracture'. As far as I know, there is no medical condition by this name. Radhamadhab probably meant Dupuytren's contracture, which is also known as *palmar fibromatosis* (which probably explains Radhamadhab's confusion about the name).

People who suffer from Dupuytren's find that their fingers bend inwards and cannot be straightened. Doctors can surgically remove the tissues that cause the condition, and then straighten the affected fingers. The doctors who examined Narayan Sanyal recommended surgery to address the condition. 'He is suffering great pain,' Radhamadhab wrote, 'and the present ailment may result in permanent damage to both of his hands.'

Radhamadhab turned to Binayak Sen, who was not just one of the state's better known doctors but also the head of the Chhattisgarh PUCL and therefore familiar with the laws and rights of prisoners. He asked Sen to visit Narayan in jail and assess his fitness for this surgery, should the Chhattisgarh government grant permission for it.

On 8 July that year, Sen wrote a letter on a Chhattisgarh PUCL letterhead to the same superintendent. 'Kindly grant permission,' he wrote, 'for me to see Shri Narayan Sanyal, who is an undertrial in your custody.'

This request was passed up through the police bureaucracy. On 6 September 2006, police officials in Raipur replied in Hindi to the superintendent: '*Central Jail Raipur mein bandi Narayan Sanyal se bhent karne ke liye Dr Binayak Sen jaata hai to is karyalay ko koi aapatti nahin hai.*' ('This department has no objection if Dr Binayak Sen goes to meet Narayan Sanyal who is detained in Central Jail, Raipur.')

With the permission thus granted, Sen started visiting Sanyal in jail.

At some point during these visits, say the police, Sen took three letters from Sanyal and passed them on to Piyush Guha, a Calcutta businessman. According to them, Guha was then going to pass these letters on to Maoists. There are questions about this narrative that I'll get to. But first, what was in the letters?

Here they are, in full:[22]

Letter #1 – original, in English

Dear Friend V

As usual you failed to your commitment of maintaining contact and help to the jail comrades. And this is nothing surprising. But it is not good.

Congress no doubt gave some boost in general. What are your personal reaction (sic) and your comrades in arms? How was the debates and its results? I got a final task. Is there any development in the work of workers and urban or in the peasantry of partially developed area. Any new initiative? What happened to urban/ working class, paper finally? There is a big gap of information and report. Would you please help? From your area there is big scope of contact. Please try to fulfill your commitment, at least partially. Why don't you send some fund to take to city friends so that they can do things. 30–50 thousand? Here all are from your area. Ok.

My health is not going well, arthritis is a new thing catching up. Age is telling. Otherwise ok. Please reply. With good wishes and R greetings to you all.
Yours

Letter #2 – original, in English

Dear P,
It is really a great success in holding and completing the ninth congress against this environment and repression. Awaiting more detail reports. Final task, it is ok.

Dear Comrade, at this juncture of the movement, we need to expand to other areas. Still our movement is confined in backward areas. The vast peasantry with main issues other than land is still uncovered and over and above workers both organize and unorganized sectors are still out of our organization. Without penetrating in these sectors, it is difficult to take the movement to the highest stage. One more important thing is propaganda. Reactionary propaganda is overwhelming peoples mind. They are able to influence peoples conceptions and thinking; knowing well that they are corrupt and anti people. Doing all for few and themselves. Our mistakes and inefficiency they propagate in a great way. One day recently TV showed one Jan Adalat where our armed squad was beating 2/3 people for acknowledging their guilt. No role of people. This I think reactionary TV person in flicked and taken shots, convincing our lower ranks.

I feel vast information gap (I feel). It is natural, but please do (help) something. To my understanding, although there is already serious political and economic crisis, in not only Imperialist camp, but also in other countries. Great divide between few rich and vast poor is unprecedented now. But development of positive political force in the world is completely absent. More in advance countries. And few positive force is unable to develop any front or able to penetrate in the middle force. Those want to oppose Imperialist/capitalist/ misdeeds. No doubt people has serious resentment/ opposition to Imperialist Capitalism, but no penetrating movement is taking place. What happened to our plan for International organizational penetration. Is there any development with Nepal taking the permanent way to parliament? I feel that international organization has collapsed.

Other section of people where our struggle is very weak. We must take special initiative to penetrate.

Otherwise it is difficult to sustain even. Change of issue when partial socio-economic change is taking place. With globalization, many new and real issues are coming. We should/must develop some infrastructure to catch up those. Or we would be able to develop. Sorry so many things I am writing all you know. And must be trying a real difficult task.

Otherwise I am ok. Some new ailments- arthritis is coming up along with general weakness. No progress in court. This jail is pouring regularly from Rajnandgaon. MR should take some initiative. They should send some fund to friends here. More next time. With R greetings to you all.

Yours

16.4.07.

Letter #3 – translated from Bengali

Dear friend,

I hope you are well. There is no news or letter from you for a long time. I hope all is well. Please write sometimes. I am at present in Raipur. In between I was at Bilaspur. I am trying to go there. Anyway, the main part of this case is over. But for the last two and half months, there is no production in court. The advocate has been told but he is also unable to do anything. Maybe he is trying to delay. In my opinion, he is not doing anything seriously. Ask Tilak to talk. The state surely wants to delay as much as possible. I do not know what is happening about me in Giridih. I heard

> that there is still no bail application to Ranchi (HC). Why late? If there is bail there, one can take a chance, if it can be done tactfully, which I missed in AP. You discuss about this. How is your business doing? I know nothing. Has there been collection from Mangel? The Giridih matter is important and needs to be done quickly. In between I have received a letter from Saheb. He has written that he is thinking about me. Let us see. Am not getting any papers/magazines from there. Please send. Have heard reports, but have not seen anything. My love to all of you,
>
> Yours.

Again, my reaction while reading these paragraphs was, where's the crime? What is there in these letters that violates the law in Chhattisgarh? I realize that a prosecution that uses these letters as evidence will do its best to find suspicious phrases or hints of conspiracy and explain those to the court. Perhaps, they'll say, the language is all an elaborate code anyway. In fact, in the judgement that sentenced Sen to life in prison, we learn that these letters 'had been written to inspire terrorist and Naxalite activities' ('*aatankvadi, naxali gatividhiyon ko protsahit karte hue likhi gayi thi*').

The prosecution found plenty wrong with the letters, and some of that is reflected in Paragraph 94 of the judgement. Three examples below, all referring to letter #2 above (the one that begins 'Dear P'):

The judge writes that letter #2 'also calls murders reactionary' ('*saath hi hathyaon ko pratikriyavaadi hona*'). But far from calling them reactionary, Sanyal does not even use the word 'murder' in letter #2 – take a look. 'Reactionary' itself appears twice, once referring to propaganda, once to TV. What did the judge mean by the reference to murders?

The judge then writes that letter #2 'talks of reaching the Parliament via Maoists' (*'Nepal mein maovadiyon dvara seedhe parliament pahunchne ke baat kahi gayi hai'*). The line he is referring to is: 'Is there any development with Nepal taking the permanent way to parliament?' Whatever Sanyal meant by that question, how did it become 'reaching the Parliament via Maoists'?

The judge's sentence quoted above continues: '... and talks of sending some amount [of money] to somebody named 'M.R." (*'tatha kisi M.R. namak vyakti ko kucch rakam bhejne ke bare mein bhi lekh hai'*.) 'M.R.' appears nearly at the end of letter #2: 'M.R. should take some initiative. They should send some fund to friends here.' Whoever or whatever 'M.R.' is, Sanyal suggests it should send money to someone. The judgement turns this completely around, pronouncing that the letter speaks of someone sending money to 'M.R.' To my mind, this twisting of facts itself tells a story of the emptiness in the prosecution's case.

Two of the pillars that support the entire edifice of the prosecution and conviction of Binayak Sen are these: that he visited Narayan Sanyal in jail, and that he carried Sanyal's letters out of jail.

At best, these pillars are flimsy. What would the prosecution do with them? What would it do with flimsiness?

7

Charge sheets and Sheets

There was one thing they could do. They could bury the judge, the case, and all of us following it, in so much paper and so many words that nobody would care to read and comprehend them all. Think how many times you have heard that in some high-profile case – say, the 1993 Bombay bomb blast case – the prosecution submitted a charge sheet running to, say, 12,000 pages. Have you ever wondered what is actually in those pages?

I don't know how many thousands of pages were submitted to the Chhattisgarh Sessions Court to make the state's case against Binayak Sen. But I do know some of what is in those pages. Some examples:

- Letters from a particular woman to her jailed husband, 14 pages.
- A sample of the same woman's handwriting, four pages.

- A sample 'obtained from Nagpur' of the same woman's 'natural' handwriting, four pages.
- The report of a handwriting expert who examined these letters and samples, three pages.
- The report of an apparent examination of this handwriting expert, five pages.

Who this woman and her husband are is not important here, though I'll discuss them shortly. (No, it's not Sen and his wife). Nor are the contents of those letters important. It would be good to know what the distinction is between a handwriting sample and a 'natural' handwriting sample, and why the latter had to be procured from Nagpur, but those details are also unimportant here.

The point is, of all the pages that make up this charge sheet, 30 are right here, in these references to one woman's handwriting. Add to that these other examples:

- Certified copies of two magazines, 50 pages.
- Statistics of Naxalite violence, including newspaper clippings, 42 pages.
- Certified copies of FIRs and case papers from other cases in Bhadrachalam, Dantewada, Bijapur, Giridih and Burdwan, a total of 86 pages.

We have accounted for 208 pages – enough for an average Agatha Christie novel – right here, and we have not yet come to the accusations against Sen. I'm not trying to suggest that the papers I have mentioned here are completely irrelevant to the case. I'm only saying, it is hard for any judge, let alone the rest of us, to examine all these pages in every nuance and detail, to uncover aspects about them that might be confusing. This is not an aspersion on judges. This is just a statement of fact: very few of us have the time, the patience and the will to go through every one of hundreds of pages, let alone with care.

I believe the prosecution knows this. This is why they put together a dossier of documents that runs to hundreds of pages. Now they can make allegations without feeling the need to support them right there with facts, secure in the knowledge that anyone who reads the allegations will assume the facts must be somewhere – *somewhere* – in those sheets of paper. After all, isn't that what you would assume, that *somewhere* in those pages there's evidence of guilt?

It's in the light of such an assumption that we should look at the charge sheets, the supplementary documents, the evidence, the transcripts of witness cross-examinations: in short, at all the paper that's part of this prosecution of Binayak Sen.

That's a lot of looking, of course. So I'll pick and choose.

A 'Supplementary Charge sheet'[23], for example, begins with several pages that list witnesses and documents. Once those are done, the charge sheet moves on to a 'Short Description of the Incident'. The second paragraph includes this sentence: '[Sen] has been meeting the Naxals accused of murders and an accused Dheeraj Mohli, who has charges of looting diamond worth Rs. several lakhs and kidnapping of a businessman and he has been meeting Narayan Sanyal repeatedly.'

Remarkably, in the early statement of Sen's crimes lies some truth about the charges he faces. In this charge sheet, the Chhattisgarh police do not accuse Sen of murders, nor looting diamonds, nor kidnapping businessmen – all of which crimes they ascribe to unnamed Naxals and Dheeraj Mohli. Whoever wrote these sentences has just one thing he can accuse Sen of, and he wants to make something of it: that Sen 'has been meeting the Naxals'.

In their view of the world, meeting Naxals is a crime.

If it is, most of us will need to be punished. Because it's likely that in just going about our lives, we will at some point meet someone who belongs to some dreaded or maybe even banned movement. Someone like a Naxal. This is just the law of averages at work, in the same way as we will at some point meet someone from Manipur, or a Jain monk.

Or put it another way: suppose we come to be ruled by a political dispensation that decides that, just as we now abhor Naxals and Maoists, some other groups of people – the Republican Party of India, or the RSS, or India Against Corruption – are undesirable, for whatever reason. Would it be a crime to then meet someone who belongs to one of these? Would it be a crime to meet Anna Hazare?

The answer is no. You are not guilty of a crime because you meet someone. The usual phrase for this is 'guilt by association', and being a reasonable citizen, you know it can't be used to tar you.

But it's more that just *knowing* we can't presume someone guilty by association. The Supreme Court has actually pronounced itself on the idea of guilt by association. In February 2011, a Supreme Court bench of Justices Markandeya Katju and Gyan Sudha Misra ruled[24] that 'mere membership of a banned organization will not make a person a criminal unless he resorts to violence or incites people to violence.'

This is actually a more stringent condition than in Sen's case.

It must say something about Sen's prosecutors that they actually start this charge sheet with non-crimes like 'meeting the Naxals' and 'meeting Narayan Sanyal repeatedly'. It sets the tone for the rest of the charge sheet, which is filled with claims like these.

Two paragraphs later, it speaks about the woman whose handwriting I wrote about above. Her name is Shoma Sen (no relation to Binayak Sen), and she is the wife of a Tusharkanti Bhattacharya, a man who is in jail. Shoma Sen wrote some letters to her husband. These letters, the charge sheet says, 'refer to the accused Dr Binayak Sen of this case.'

'It is clear,' says the charge sheet after mentioning this, 'that Dr Binayak Sen has connections with such dreaded Naxalites.'

Here, for the prosecution, is more evidence of Sen's guilt: he is mentioned in letters written by a woman to her husband. Yet again, we have guilt by association – witness the word 'connections'. What if Shoma Sen referred to the President of India, or Nelson Mandela, or Roger Federer, or perhaps the Police Commissioner of Chhattisgarh, in her letters to her husband?

An interesting feature of the charge sheet is the number of times it says something of apparent portent, that on just a little bit of thought adds up to nothing at all. There is a prime example in the two sentences immediately after this assertion about Binayak Sen's 'connections with such dreaded Naxalites.'

In the first sentence, the police tell the court that Shoma Sen has been working as a lecturer in a Nagpur college since 1987, and took three days leave in September 2007 to go to Patna. In the second, they tell the court that all this was confirmed by the principal of the Nagpur college. After this, the charge sheet never mentions this leave taken, this Patna trip, again; not does it expain their relevance to Sen and his case. But the charge sheet does list the principal, Shri A.R. Wankhede, as a witness, saying that he will certify his statement. Which he did, when he was examined during the trial.

But what is all this about?

There is a clue, not in the charge sheet but in the judgement. Paragraph 71 of the judgement refers to Principal Wankhede's appearance in court as a witness. It speaks of Tusharkanti Bhattacharya's arrest in Patna in September 2007. Presumably that accounts for the three days of leave that Shoma Sen asked her principal for: that is, now we know why she travelled to Patna.

But what the connection is to Binayak Sen, or how this serves to establish his guilt beyond just mentions of him in letters, remains unclear.

So far, we have looked at only the first four paragraphs in this 'Short Description of the Incident', and already there have been plenty of questions. But there are more.

Two paragraphs later is an excellent example of another tactic that's been commonly used in this case. It refers to a magazine called *Prabhat,* 'seized from accused Piyush Guha'. There's a short run-through of some of what's in *Prabhat* that the prosecution finds offensive. We learn that it talks of a boycott of the Lok Sabha elections, pushing the 'people's war', 'strengthening the guerilla Army', an attack on the Bailadila Explosives Depot that killed 'five Army men and wounded another nine' and 'other dangerous objectives.'

Alarming stuff indeed. Immediately after this run-through, we read: 'Like this accused Piyush Guha together with Dr Binayak Sen with directions from Narayan Sanyal was working for the Maoist organization.'

There is no connection made between the contents of *Prabhat* and the three accused men, nothing that justifies the use of that phrase 'like this' to start this sentence, nothing that shows that they were 'working for the Maoist organization.' *Nothing.*

But we are only a third of the way through this paragraph. There are nearly 200 words left to read, and describing as they do the crimes of Maoists, they make dismal reading. The Maoists destroy public property like schools and bridges. Their main objective is to murder innocent women, children and government servants. They have no other work but destruction and bomb blasts and looting. They are very dangerous and are creating an atmosphere of terror all over the country. They don't have faith in the rule of law, and in Chhattisgarh they are routinely murdering people and burning things.

It's a breathless, repetitive passage that does well to capture something of the Chhattisgarh administration's fear of Maoists, even the horrific spectre this movement has mutated into. This is underlined in the first several lines in the following paragraph, which talks of a battle between CRPF men and Naxalites in Dantewada. Afterward, authorities recovered much material from the site, including copies of *Prabhat* and a photograph of Narayan Sanyal sitting with members of the Maoist 'politburo'.

More grist to the mill, in other words, of those who warn of the Maoist menace.

But lest we forget: this is not a document that's meant to explain that Maoists pose a great threat to Chhattisgarh and India. This is a charge sheet filed in court against men accused under various sections of the Indian Penal Code. Therefore, it should spell out the crimes these men are accused of committing.

Yet what has happened instead? Whoever drew up this charge sheet has used several hundred words to tell us how bad the Maoists are, the crimes they commit, the terror they spread – and somewhere in the middle of that, we find the name 'Binayak Sen'. Not connected to anything, but just there, together with the unsupported claim that he works for the Maoists.

This is guilt by suggestion, guilt by the hope that when a random reader stumbles across names in the middle of a lengthy censure of Maoists, this random reader will naturally assume that those names are Maoist as well. Speak long enough of the menace of Maoists, mention Binayak Sen's name every now and then, and in the listener's mind the guilt for their crimes eventually sticks to Sen too.

Judging by what's happened to Sen, and by all that's been written about him, it's an effective tactic.

The 'Short Description of the Incident' goes on for 22 paragraphs. One of those deals with bank accounts. Eighteen account numbers are mentioned; at least one account is referenced without a number. (Numerous telephone numbers and rupee amounts also make appearances.)

The barrage of numbers gets confusing, and it's not clear what their connection is to the case anyway. Bear with me while I try to make sense of it.

For example, there's a mention of 'the account number of Rupantar 9843' (Rupantar being the name of an organization Binayak and Ilina Sen ran, of which more later). Two sentences later, we read this: 'In the account number SB 01009843 there were Rs. 4,85,436 as on 23.06.07.' Three sentences later there's this: 'In the account of Rupantar account number SB/01/009843 Rs. 16,58,312 are there as on 23.06.07.'

Two different amounts in the same account on the same day.

Another account appears three times in one sentence, like this: 'account number 6176 of Binayak Sen ... second

Rupantar number 6176 ... and Ilina Sen account number 6176 are written.'

Three different holders of account 6176: Binayak Sen, Ilina Sen and Rupantar.

Account SB/01/0018289 makes appearances in successive sentences: 'Account number SB/01/0018289 in the name of Rupantar trust has been closed. In the account of Dr Binayak Sen account number SB/01/0018289 there were Rs. 41,841 as on 21.07.07.'

Is Account SB/01/0018289 closed, or is it active? Does it belong to Rupantar or to Binayak Sen?

One account, remember, is referenced without a number: 'An account in the name of Shankar Singh, Pallavi Bihar, Rohnipuram was opened on 3.11.03, in which Rs. 62,754 are there, and which has telephone number of the Rupantar organization of Dr Binayak Sen 2537542 and 2224686, in which Rs. 51,185 were there as on 28.05.07.'

How much money is in this account? 62,754 rupees? Or 51,185 rupees?

The paragraph goes on to make some remarks about Binayak Sen's profession and properties, and then there's this sentence: 'Dr Binayak Sen does not have any other source of income, still he has so much of money deposited in his accounts.' This echoes what the previous paragraph says about Sen: 'in whose banks lakhs of rupees are there.'

It also matches – or maybe it doesn't – a claim about some of these same accounts in another Supplementary Charge sheet[25]: that they contain 'money over Rs. 40,000 lakh.' That's Rs 400 crore. Is the Chhattisgarh government really suggesting that Sen has stashed away in these banks an amount six times as large as that involved in the Bofors scandal? Does it really believe that this confusing hailstorm of account and telephone numbers constitutes proof of that suggestion?

If you look closely, the sole reference to a rupee amount that the charge sheet claims actually belongs to Sen is the one mentioned above, SB/01/0018289: 'In the account of Dr Binayak Sen account number SB/01/0018289 there were Rs 41,841 as on 21.07.07.' That's the only reference, and if you remember the sentence immediately preceding this one in the charge sheet claims the account belongs to Rupantar and is closed.

In any case, is the prosecution really describing this sum of Rs 41,841 as 'so much of money', and 'lakhs of rupees', and maybe even '40,000 lakh' rupees?

What about the phone numbers? To go with claims about money, the charge sheet says Sen was 'using 8–10 phone numbers, many mobile numbers'; and later, that 'he has been using tens of phone numbers, what is the purpose of these, it is a serious and worrying issue.'

The only phone numbers mentioned in the charge sheet come in pairs: 2537542 and 2224686 (described as 'telephone number of the Rupantar organization of Dr Binayak Sen'), 2262260 and 2424689 ('the phone numbers of their residence') and 2422857 and 2510539. Exactly six numbers, and as best as I can tell, not a mobile among them. These six, the charge sheet describes as '8–10 phone numbers' and 'tens of phone numbers'.

This is indeed a serious and worrying issue.

In the same paragraph, we are told that 'it is clear that Binayak Sen has been collecting money' for Naxalites. Elsewhere, we find that 'it is clear that for the purpose of running Naxalite organization, a secret role has been played by Binayak Sen.' That 'it is clear that Dr Binayak Sen has connections with such dreaded naxalites.' That 'it is clear that Dr Binayak Sen is directly connected to the banned Maoist organization.'

Juxtapose all this supposed clarity, a little further in the charge sheet, with still more numbers. These tell us about Maoist depredations: 291 vehicles destroyed, 75 road bridges destroyed, 87 school buildings destroyed, and much more. All also serious and worrying. But no connection between these abominations and Sen is even mentioned, let alone spelled out. Like with much else in this prosecution, you are meant to infer that he bears guilt, somehow, for these crimes.

The only thing that is clear, then, is the degree of obfuscation in this charge sheet.

8

Insinuation

Where evidence and charges are flimsy at best, you might expect to find insinuation. With Sen's case, you will not be disappointed.

In charge sheets filed against Sen you will find these lines:

> *'Dr Vinayak [sic] Sen dacter avashya hain, parantu dacteri peshe ke naam par woh shunya hain. Iske ghar ki talaashi ke dauran na to wahan dacter ke clinic jaise koi cheez dikhi aur na hi koi dawa wagarah rakhi hui payi gayi.'*
> (Dr Binayak Sen is certainly a doctor, but in terms of the practice of medicine is a zero. During the search of his house nothing was found that would appear in a doctor's clinic, nor were there any medicines there.)
>
> 'On 19.05.07 when Dr Binayak Sen's house was searched, none of the following were found in

his treatment room – a table to treat the patients, stethoscope, medicines, BP machine, register with the treatment of patients and a time table to meet the patients. Dr Binayak Sen is a doctor only by name, there is no treatment.'

If the prosecution can undermine Sen's claim to be a doctor, it can legitimately ask, just who is this person? What are his qualifications to be in rural Chhattisgarh, doing what he is doing? In fact, what exactly is he doing? Under the cloak of treating patients, isn't he actually helping Maoists and waging war against the country?

When the charge sheet says 'Dr Sen is a doctor only by name', and remarks on the absence of medical gadgets in his house, these are exactly the questions that arise.

Of course not all doctors work from their homes, or have their working paraphernalia at home. I know some of the doctors at a rural clinic called Jan Swasthya Sahyog in Ganiyari, Chhattisgarh, and have been in their home several times. They too have no stethoscopes or BP machines lying around at home. In other words, this strange accusation could easily have been made about them too. Yet I have seen them at work, in the clinic in Ganiyari, in their outreach clinics in small villages like Bamhni and Bokrakachhar. There, they see patients who have been waiting patiently for them. They use stethoscopes and BP machines. They fill registers with their observations, perform surgeries, prescribe drugs and treatment, bring babies into the world. They save lives.

It would be a travesty to say of these people, merely

by looking around their homes and failing to find medical equipment, that they are doctors '*only by name*' and '*there is no treatment*' that they perform.

But for those who are persuaded by this accusation anyway, who find it hard to believe that Sen is actually a doctor, consider some handwritten records from a clinic he ran in a village called Bagrumnala.[26] Handwritten, that is, by Sen.

Of one patient he examined, Sen wrote: 'Abd: No tenderness. No shifting dullness. No masses felt. Rx Hydrochlorothiazide, 1 tab od × 7.'[27]

Whatever this patient complained of, on examination Sen found no tenderness in the abdomen, or masses, etc. Therefore, Sen prescribed one tablet of hydrochlorothiazide a day for a week. This drug is a diuretic, often prescribed for patients who complain of fluid retention or high blood pressure. Perhaps this patient came to Bagrumnala suffering from a distended abdomen.

On 20 February 2007 – only three months before he was arrested – Sen examined another patient in Bagrumnala and wrote this in the records: 'Pain L testis mild. Doxycycline 100 mg bd x 5 days. Paracetamol 1 tab [illegible] x 5 days. Hetrazan 100 mg [illegible] × 7 days.'[28]

The patient had pain in his left testis. Sen gave him paracetamol for the pain and to ward off any fever, and two different drugs to address the possible causes of the pain in the man's testis. Doxycycline is typically used to treat elephantiasis, a condition that results in permanently swollen limbs and genitals. It is also useful in treating the sexually transmitted disease chlamydia, among whose symptoms are swollen, tender testicles. Hetrazan (a trade name for Diethylcarbamazine, or DEC) is prescribed for patients suffering from lymphatic filariasis, a disease caused by the parasite *Wuchereria bancrofti*, whose most obvious symptom is elephantiasis.

One week later – 27 February 2007 – the same patient returned to Bagrumnala. He had clearly followed Sen's prescribed treatment and his condition had improved. Sen must have concluded that he had lymphatic filariasis and not chlamydia, and therefore dropped the Doxycycline and prescribed a further course of Hetrazan. This was what Sen wrote after examining him that day: 'Better. Hetrazan 100 mg bd × 14.'

Better, but not well enough yet to stop the treatment.

Who but a trained doctor could have made these examinations and diagnoses, prescribed these drugs, and then written these notes in the register in Bagrumnala? Who but a doctor would be able to conclude after a follow-up examination that the patient was 'better' and therefore could stop taking some of the drugs prescribed earlier?

And who would look at these notes, the patient records they speak of, and still conclude that because Sen's home had no stethoscope or BP machine, he must be a 'doctor only by name'? That he did 'no treatment' of any real patients? Did the prosecution look at these Bagrumnala records at all?

Why ignore this abundant evidence of treatment? Why mock Sen's medical credentials?

What makes the mockery more perverse is something the Chhattisgarh State Government did in 2003. On 3 April that year, the secretary of the state Health and Family Welfare Department, Dr Alok Shukla, signed an 'order' ('*aadesh*'), which, in translation, read thus:

> The State Government has undertaken a comprehensive programme of reforms in Health Sector in pursuance of Sector Investment programme of the Central Government. For this purpose the State Government has constituted a State Advisory Committee for bringing changes in the State policies, structural changes in law and procedural programmes as mentioned in the Annexure. This committee will perform the function of a mediator between the committee and the people at large for betterment of health policies and radical reconstruction of health sector.
>
> Following members have been nominated to the Committee.

The order then lists 17 names. At #9 in that list: 'Dr Binayak Sen, Rupantar'. At #11: 'Dr Ilina Sen, Rupantar'.[29]

Why would the Chhattisgarh government appoint to this advisory committee a man it believes to be a 'doctor only in name'? Why would it also appoint to the same committee a woman, his wife, whom it accuses of helping Naxalites?

9

Interlude: What Development Means

On a recent trip to Chhattisgarh, I visited a village called Bamhni. The Jan Swasthya Sahyog (JSS) of Ganiyari, outside Bilaspur, runs an outreach clinic there. Every Tuesday, one or two JSS doctors and a small team of health workers get into a Mahindra Bolero in Ganiyari and drive an hour-and-a-half to reach Bamhni. Waiting for them there are the village health workers JSS has trained and a few dozen patients. This is really the only accessible health care for a cluster of several Baiga tribal villages in the surrounding degraded forest.

There was a workshop that day for *dais*, usually older women from the villages who help with childbirth and maternity issues. Perhaps two dozen had arrived for the workshop; several of them had walked ten kilometres to get here. There was also the usual collection of patients waiting patiently to see doctors about an illness, or a wound, or a chronic condition. The weekly clinic is about their only chance to see a doctor and they must make the most of it.

I spent much of the day with an even smaller JSS team that reaches out even beyond this outreach clinic. The area we were in is part of the Achanakmar Wildlife Sanctuary, which has existed since the mid-70s. As happens with several Indian wildlife reserves, this one has several villages located inside its boundaries. In 2009, Achanakmar was declared part of Project Tiger, the more stringent Indian effort to save that splendid animal. More stringent, that is, in the conditions it spells out for villages in designated sanctuaries. When Achanakmar joined Project Tiger, the residents of Bamhni and several other villages were told they would have to move out of the 'core zone' of the sanctuary, so as to leave the tigers an area where they would be undisturbed.

We were going that day to two villages that were 'resettled' outside the core zone close to a year earlier. This was considered a model resettlement effort: forest officials regularly brought recalcitrant residents from other core zone villages here to give them the message, 'This is what you will get, if you agree to move.' For this reason, when the smaller team announced that they were going to these villages, I jumped at the chance to accompany them. I wanted to see how this resettlement had happened.

The villages are now two long rows of identical pista-icecream-green concrete blocks, identically spaced and lined up with razor-sharp precision. Between the rows is a concrete road. There are plenty of trees on the hillsides behind the village, and on either side of the road leading there. But once you reach the concrete blocks, there is not a single tree, and thus no shade at all. It was unpleasant enough to walk from house to house on a blazing March afternoon. April and May promised worse.

The residents of Bokrakachhar, one of the two villages, sat in front of their own particular concrete blocks, in the shadow of the parapets overhead. In the houses across the road, the angle of the sun meant there wasn't even that much shade. On the walls behind the villagers, I could see neatly wired electrical fittings – switches, plugs, fan regulators, even a glimpse of a fan inside one house. Why, I wondered, weren't these people inside with the fan on? Why were they out here at all?

I asked 30 year-old Aghan Singh, whom I met outside his home, those questions. He looked at me in surprise. 'There's no electricity', he said. 'You mean, there's no electricity right now?' I asked. 'There's a power cut? When does the power return?' Aghan was shaking his head even as I spoke. 'No, there's no electricity! We've never had electricity!'

Bokrakachhar's residents' new houses were wired up nicely for electricity, down to panels on the wall with arrays of switches and sockets, even the occasional fan. But a year after moving in, they still didn't have electricity.

But there were more woes. There's no piped water in these houses. There are just two handpumps provided in the village. There are no schools, no health clinic, no transport. If villagers here need to travel to Bamhni for the Tuesday JSS outreach clinic, let's say, they must walk about one-and-a-half kilometres to a tarred road, where occasional buses ply.

To me, this model of Achanakmar resettlement is just two rows of sun-seared concrete without a soul, without evidence that those who built this place had much of a soul. Perhaps the villagers will plant trees and eventually make Bokrakachhar a more livable community than it was that hot March morning. But considering it was a settlement built from scratch, why did nobody think of a health clinic? Why not supply water to the houses? Why not give them electricity? Why go through the charade of actually wiring up the houses?

One final note from Bokrakachhar. The Chhattisgarh government has a programme under which people below the poverty line (BPL) can buy 35 kilograms of rice a month, at a price of Rs 3 per kg. Plenty of families qualify for this programme. But plenty also cannot afford even the Rs 3 price. The government paints red rectangles outside the doors of such homes to show that they are eligible to buy rice at Rs 1 per kg. These little red rectangles were plentiful – at times nearly ubiquitous – in Bamhni and other villages I have visited in the area, Bokrakachhar no exception.

Aghan Singh showed me his red 'ration card', which said he had been buying rice at one rupee per kg every month since August 2007. His most recent purchase had been just three days before I met him.

My head filled with all kinds of questions as I strolled through Bokrakachhar licking an ice-lolly I paid an itinerant vendor a rupee for, as the JSS team did what they had come to do. Yes, I couldn't help noting that I paid the same for this ice-lolly, without even thinking about it, as Aghan Singh paid for a kilo of rice.

From Bokrakachhar, we drove to another resettled village, Bahaud. Similar razor-sharp rows of pista-coloured blocks, though here a few bare trees broke the monotony. The JSS staff set up their equipment in the porch of one of the houses, then fanned out through the village asking the pregnant women to meet them for their weekly check-up. I spoke with a young volunteer.

The house opposite was used as an *anganwadi*, a child-care centre, she said, and under another government programme, children there got midday meals. But for weeks, no grain had been supplied to make the meal. So the *anganwadi* no longer operated.

Meanwhile, perhaps ten pregnant women had formed a line to meet the Ganiyari team. One by one, they had their height and weight recorded, spoke quietly to the health worker, gave blood and urine samples to be tested. I was not really paying attention to all this, chatting instead with a gaggle of kids.

Until I noticed, with a start, who was doing the testing. It was a man called Ajay. He sat on a mat in a corner of the porch. In turn, the women squatted in front of him and held out their arms. He pulled a needle from his bag, felt for a vein, inserted the needle and drew a syringe-full of blood. He emptied it into a tiny bottle, asked the woman her name, wrote it on a little label that he pasted on the bottle. Next, he gave the woman a shallow plastic cup and motioned for her to go behind the house. She got up, walked behind and returned a few minutes later with a little urine sloshing around in the cup. Ajay carefully poured a little into a test-tube and added a chemical, observing just as carefully what transpired in the tube. Then he made a note on a chart.

Ajay is trained well. He churns through this delicate little routine with efficiency, discretion and a minimum of fuss.

He is also the man who drove us here in the Mahindra Bolero.

There's no reason a JSS driver cannot double up as a sample-taker and pathologist, and in fact it makes the task of outreach that much simpler if people in your team can wear multiple hats. Simple good sense. And yet, something about this situation – that in this resettled village, these pregnant women were being tested by the driver of a Bolero – something about it amounted to a commentary on health care in these parts. Which pregnant woman in our cities, I wonder, has had her vital signs checked similarly?

When the team was finally done monitoring the pregnant women, they packed their equipment and filled the back of the Bolero with it. The gaggle of kids clustered around, all gap-toothed smiles and waves. Ajay started the engine and we were about to move, when there was a small commotion and fingers pointed down the road, to two women hurrying towards us.

Our two women volunteers got out of the car to speak to them. By now, we could see that one was carrying a tiny baby, her *pallu* wrapped protectively over its head. The four women met in the middle of the road, and a long animated conversation ensued in Chhattisgarhi. We left after a ten-minute delay.

Back in the Bolero, the JSS women told us what happened. Only three weeks old, the baby had developed pneumonia. It had been several days now, and the mother was beside herself with worry. The volunteers reassured her, saying they had left some appropriate and low-cost medicines with the local health worker. If the child had not recovered by next Tuesday, they told her, she should bring her to Bamhni to meet the JSS doctor.

'How will she reach Bamhni?' I asked.

'Someone in the village will give her a ride on a motorbike or a bullock-cart,' said the volunteer. 'Otherwise she will walk.'

'How far is it to Bamhni?' I asked as we drove on.

'Not that far. About eight or ten kilometres,' the volunteer said.

I was thinking, as we drove, of a young woman carrying a *pallu*-wrapped pneumonia-stricken newborn eight or ten kilometres to Bamhni next Tuesday.

That was my second visit to Bamhni and its surrounds. The first was a year earlier, when I had come with a JSS team that included Dr Yogesh Jain, one of the doctors who founded the organization in the late 1990s.

That Tuesday, one of the patients waiting to see Dr Jain was a painfully thin man, his arms and legs like sticks. I found it difficult even to look at him. It was a visible effort for him even to step onto a weighing machine that was raised four inches off the ground. The dial showed us his weight: 28.9 kg. At nearly six feet tall and fifty-five years old, Dhanga Baiga weighed ten kg less than my ten-year-old son. Dhanga suffered from TB and – it was the JSS doctors who got me into the habit of describing this one as a disease – chronic hunger.

Dr Jain was in a small room lit by a shaft of sunlight, examining patients one by one. After weighing himself, Dhanga walked in there slowly, haltingly. I don't like being a voyeur with doctors and their patients. But now I could not help looking in as he sat with this doctor who might have been from another planet, for all the world like a father wasting away and his son trying to reassure him. In the soft, calm tone Dr Jain used to speak to him, in Dhanga's air of resignation, in the gentle hand Dr Jain placed on Dhanga's knee, I sensed the quiet bond between these two men.

My companion on that trip was the photographer Tom Pietrasik. He took a picture of Dhanga weighing himself. JSS used that portrait of knobby legs and claw-like hands on the cover of their annual report, published a few months later. It had this caption: 'Dhanga Baiga, 55 years-old, suffering from tuberculosis and chronic hunger. Weighs 28 kilos. Body Mass Index 10.9, considered too low to be compatible with life.'

Those last few words were prophetic. I did not see Dhanga on my second visit to Bamhni. Back in Ganiyari that evening after returning from Bokrakachhar and Bamhni, I ran into

Dr Jain. 'Hey, we just heard,' he told me softly. 'Dhanga died last night.'

Why is all this relevant to Binayak Sen? One reason is the connection between Sen and JSS: he is on their advisory board, knows their doctors, and they have worked hard to defend him in his case.

But it's not the only reason. As with the man and his daughters whom I spent a day with in Mankhurd, stories like those at Bamhni and Bokrakachhar have lessons for how India has developed and how that development has affected people.

Bokrakachhar speaks clearly of the way we have approached the process of resettlement. In this case of course, the village was displaced by a tiger reserve; but people have been displaced like that not just with wildlife reserves, but with any number of dams (Sardar Sarovar) and power projects (Enron). It's nobody's case that displacement itself must never happen – that is clearly an impossibility. But surely it is conceivable that those displaced are treated with a minimum dignity and respect? Surely this principle is not unreasonable: that people displaced in the name of progress and development must end up with at least a noticeably better quality of life than they had before?

Instead, an official cynicism says we can do anything we want with the lives of these people. They live so far off the beaten track, so removed from the national consciousness, that nobody will even know, let alone care, what happens to them. We can make grandiloquent claims (like, maybe, 'the new village is electrified') about generous rehabilitation policies, confident that few who hear such claims will actually step out to verify their authenticity. And when some actually do step out, their observations can be dismissed as the biased remarks of 'outsiders', or 'socialists', or 'busybodies', or '*jholawallas*'.

Or 'Maoists'.

To me, the Maoist spectre across the middle of this country is not so much about violence, or injustices done to tribals by the Salwa Judum. It is about the attitude in us that makes Maoist violence possible, that makes people turn to Maoists for help in solving their problems. It is about a profound indifference to the way many Indians live. It is about the glazed look that even a few paragraphs about far-off villages in a remote part of Chhattisgarh will bring about.

The interesting and important question is not why the Maoists take to violence, but why they attract so much support. For the Maoists could not flourish, as they do across a broad belt of India, without widespread support from people in those areas.

Why do they get that support?

Unless India finds the honesty and will to tackle that question, I believe we are doomed to a never-ending battle with the Maoist insurgency, with no guarantee of success. And a good first step towards that finding that will is to understand the reality of places like Bamhni, Bokrakachhar and Bahaud.

10

Look at the Evidence

Nothing says quite as much about a court case – or, which might amount to the same thing, about the prosecution's faith in its case in court – as the material the prosecution offers to support its case. I've considered some of that before in this book. Here's some more.

On 19 May 2007, a few days after his first arrest, the Chhattisgarh police visited Sen's home in Raipur and seized his computer. They sent it on to the Central Forensic Science Laboratory (CFSL) in Hyderabad. Between the police and the lab, they found and printed nearly 350 pages of material from the computer. These, they compiled into two spiral-bound books, with smart covers.

One says this on the cover: 'TO HONORABLE (*sic*) SUPREME COURT, NEW DELHI. The details of the print out taken from CD/DVD, which is seized from the computer and CPU of Dr Binayak Sen ... On date 19/05/2007'.

The other cover is in Hindi. Under the heading '*Thana Ganj Zila Raipur*' and the case numbers, it says: '*INDEX: Aaropi Vinayak* (sic) *Sen se japt aath CD ke print out ki sankshipt vivaranika*' ('A concise analysis of the print out of eight CDs confiscated from accused Binayak Sen').

Both books have lists at the beginning describing the contents, document by document. There you will see entries such as 'Code Names of Ilina Sen, Binayak Sen and others', 'Reference of a letter of Com Kusumlata mentioned by Dr Ilina Sen' and 'Appeal from the National President (PUCL), People War Group, Maoist Community Centre, Naxalite, POTA-Like Laws'. Other entries contain names and phrases like 'ISI', 'Banned organization' and 'PAKISTAN'.

For anyone who reads the tables of contents in these books, some of these entries would seem damning indeed. Others, though, would seem bafflingly mundane.

Code Names

Looking at the tables, you cannot help wondering, what kind of man is this Binayak Sen anyway, who harbours all this nefarious material on his computer? And why are he and 'others' using code names? Which is exactly how the Chhattisgarh police wanted you, and the judge of the sessions court, to think. They probably did not expect anyone to go beyond the contents and actually read the documents themselves. The contents, they thought, would be enough. Because if you actually did read the documents ...

Start with the code names. Here is the page, in its entirety, that the index entry refers to:

APARIJITA SEN (BILLO)
PRANHITA SEN (LALI)
ILINA SEN (RIMI)
BINAYAK SEN (RANA)
RUSTAM (RUSU, BHAU, & DOO)
RAUNAQ (BABI, BABNA, & RANKO)
SUROTI (SURO)
SUA (SUBUAA)
TIPU SULTAN (TUKLI, TUKU)
BADAL (BADLU, BALLI, HAJJAM)
SHIVNATH (SHIBOO, SHIVENDRA, SHIVI)
NAINA (NINUA)
MADHURI (MADHU)
SIKANDAR
NEPOLIAN
MEENAKSHI
ROMEAL
SHRIDEVI
MADHUBALA

In its entirety.

Time was when I subscribed for a few years to *The Statesman* from Calcutta, only so I could pore over its classifieds in search of sundry greetings and obits. This occasioned despair in my wife, who had to cope with the mountains of extra unread newspapers around the house while I merely clipped the particularly fascinating bits from the classifieds. I could not imagine who would not find this fascinating: '*Babi-Ma/Monima (Satyabrata and Madhulika Bose) – Congratulations on completing 36 years of wedded life and heading for the Diamond. A big thanks for being such wonderful parents and grands – Bappa, Soma, Buria, Buro, Gabbu, Jhumpi, Gupi, Buri, Gali, Mampu, Bimbi, Tuti, Tinda, Ghanta and Chhorda.*'

Yes, I have changed the names, and yes, I have it filed away somewhere, this little ode to the wonderful Bengali habit of going by nicknames. Breathes there an Indian who does not know of it?

And that's all that this page printed from Sen's computer is. Binayak Sen and family, authentic Bengalis all, go by nicknames, as all authentic Bengalis do. His wife Ilina is Rimi. His daughters Aparajita and Pranhita are Billo and Lali. He himself is Rana. (Not mentioned here is that his brother Dipankar is Tapan.) Must have happened like this: one day, somebody sat at this computer and typed up the names and nicknames of the Sen family and various others.

Why this person did this is unimportant. Consider only how the Chhattisgarh police chose to refer to this list of nicknames: 'Code Names of Ilina Sen, Binayak Sen and others'. When you accuse someone of helping Maoists, it doesn't hurt to fire off a mention of 'Code Names', with all the attendant connotations of conspiracy and underhanded dealings. Never mind that they are actually nicknames.

Of course I have no proof that these are not actually code names. All I have to compare with are my memories and clippings from *The Statesman*. If they scream to me that

'Rimi' and 'Rana' are just more in the same vein as 'Gabbu' and 'Ghanta', that's certainly not good enough to persuade a court of the innocence of this list of names. So if this was the sole document the prosecution offered to support its case, I might agree that it deserved some attention, especially because the case is about conspiracy and suspicious activities. Though equally, if this was the sole document the prosecution offered, a judge might have dismissed the case for want of any substantial evidence. Either way, we should look at the other documents produced as evidence against Sen.

The ISI and a Chimpanzee

But of course this list of names was not the sole document produced as evidence. Here's another:

> To Walter Fernandez, ISI New Delhi.
> Dear Walter,
> I wonder if you can still use this. I had to rush off to see my mother who was seriously ill after your fax came. We had sent this earlier by courier but apparently your office did not receive it. Extremely sorry for the problems you must have faced.
> warm regards and best wished (*sic*) for 1999.
> Ilina

What do you make of this? Probably what I did: that Ilina Sen sent Walter Fernandez a document which did not reach him, and she was now sending it again with a cover note. Nothing of any significance. Only, the prosecution called it 'A letter of Dr Ilina Sen to Walter Fernandez, addressing him as ISI'.

When you accuse someone of helping dangerous Maoist insurgents, it doesn't hurt to include a mention of the ISI, the Pakistani chimera that all Indians live in dread of. In fact, as the *Hindu* reported, chief prosecutor T.C. Pandya even told the court during the proceedings in the case: 'We do not know who this Fernandez is, but ISI, as we all know, means Pakistan.'[30]

It also doesn't hurt to leave out the detail that the letter is addressed to 'ISI *New Delhi*'. For otherwise someone might point out that this ISI is actually the Indian Social Institute, an over 60-year-old institution at the corner of Bhishma Pitamah Marg and Lodhi Road in New Delhi, a place where I once stayed while attending a conference in that city. Someone might point out that its director in the late 1990s – clearly when the letter was written – was a man called Walter Fernandes (not, incidentally, Fernandez).

So far, then, we have Code Names and a link sought to be made to Pakistan's ISI. Sinister in the suggestion, innocuous once you take the time to look at them, but still just two out of nearly 300 pages. Perhaps there is incriminating stuff in the other 298 pages? Consider this printout of an email message:

From: 'Ganguli, Mary'
To: 'Ilina Sen'

Date: Wed, 04 Sep 2002 16:21:13 IST
Hi, Rimi and Binayak...

yes, I can hear you; in the immortal words of Victor Raj, 'are you able to follow me?'

great to be in touch with you at last; welcome to the twenty-first century etc. I am copying this to Rohan, Shahnaz, Ranjan, Honor and Shiv.

What's new with you? our main problem is we have a chimpanzee in the white house.

Mary

—-Original Message—-

From: ilina sen

Sent: 9/4/2002 1:50AM

ddear (*sic*) mary, a few aeons ago i had received a letter from you and had sent a reply in hard copy, as well as a short note to ranjan. i dont know if you received any of this as i didn't hear from you again. we have since sorted out some of our connectivity problems and are keen to get back in touch with all of you. unfortunately your's is the only address i possess. i don't have any recent news about any of you. can you hear me out there? if so please shout back and soon. yours, binayak and rimi

What we can tell from this exchange is that in September 2002, Ilina Sen wrote a message to someone called Mary Ganguli, trying to re-establish contact with her. (Note that she signed using her 'code name', 'Rimi'; it seems clear this is an old friendship.) The same day, Ganguli, evidently happy to hear from Ilina, replied. Evidently, too, Ganguli is not much of an admirer of the then-President of the USA, George W. Bush. So she says in her email, 'We have a chimpanzee in the white house.' Not a compliment, to be sure, but hardly different from words all of us use every day to describe politicians we don't care for; and in any case, there's no law I know of that makes it illegal to call a president, even President Bush, a chimpanzee.

But of course, Ms Ganguli had no idea that this throwaway phrase would one day be used to damn Binayak Sen. This email message is listed in the contents thus: 'An email from Mary Ganguli to Dr Binayak and Rimi saying, A Chimpanzee is living in White House.' At the same time that he made a fuss about the ISI, prosecutor Pandya read out this line too, telling the sessions court in Chhattisgarh: 'This email has been written in code. It is significant because terrorists oppose the US President.'

For prosecutor Pandya, the mention of the ISI, and then a chimpanzee in the White House, 'prove that Dr Sen and his wife Ilina were part of an international terror network.'[31]

It is hard for me to believe that any reasonable prosecutor would actually seek to make a case like this, about an 'international terror network', from 'evidence' like this. Yet that is precisely what prosecutor Pandya did.

It is harder still for me to believe that any reasonable judge would listen to this and take it seriously.

But we are talking about three hundred pages, let's remember, and we've looked at just three of them.

Big Boss

This next piece of evidence is somewhat beyond comprehension.

> From: big@boss.com
> To: <rimi221@rediffmail.com>
> Date: Mon, 23 Jun 2003 10:53:27 IST
> [*No body to this message*]
> Attachment: Document003.pif (65.54 KB)

This is a message of the kind everyone who uses email has received by the score. You quickly learn that if you try to look at the document attached, you'll let a virus loose on your computer, so you learn as well to ignore and usually delete such messages.

But Ilina Sen left it in her Inbox, and that led to this entry on the contents page of this book of evidence from Sen's computer: 'An email from big@boss.com written to rimi221@rediffmail.com (Dr Ilina Sen email Id).'

Why?

Cry Wolf

Then there's this letter.

> [*The Sens' address in Raipur*]
> The General Maneger (*sic*)
> Scholastic India
> [*address in Gurgaon*]

26-Dec-2K.
Dear Sir.
Subject: To order two of your books.
I would like to buy 2 of your books – CRY WOLF & MOON BRIDGE, Which I saw at your Exhibition at RAJGHAT BESANT SCHOOL, VARANASI.
Kindly send them to me, by VPP at the address given above. Please endure (*sic*) your bill.
Thanks.
Yours sincerely,
Pranhita Sen

In 2000, when this letter was written, Pranhita, Binayak and Ilina Sen's older daughter, was a student at the Rajghat Besant School (a J. Krishnamurti school) in Varanasi. At a book exhibition, she saw two books that she wanted. She wrote to the publisher to order them. End of story.

What kind of evidence does this constitute? What did the police find suspicious in it? Yet it is there, one of the documents submitted to the court as evidence, one of the 300 pages, though without an entry in the contents page.

Government's Own

Another document found on Sen's computer:

Mahila Kosh
Traditionally, women in Chhattisgarh have a comparatively higher status with in (*sic*) families and in the society

Compared to the national gender ratio of 933 women to 1000 men, for Chhattisgarh the ratio is 900. Third after Kerala and Pondicherry.

Women constitute 36.5% of the working population among main workers

We have conceived Indira Mahila Kosh as a small yet significant gesture in order to trigger the latent potential among our women to contribute to the building of a new Chhattisgarh

The KOSH has been created with an initial corpus of Rs 1 crore [underlining done by hand]

The Governing body is headed by Minister for Women and Child Development

(A few more details about this Mahila Kosh, omitted here.)

So here we have some kind of programme or organization that we have to assume Sen established, and he did so with that '*initial corpus of Rs 1 crore*'. That phrase was actually underlined by hand on the page, and the entry in the contents makes sure the point is driven home: '*Mahila Kosh budget shows Rs 1 cr. And its detailing.*'

How did Sen, a paediatrician in rural Chhattisgarh, get this kind of money?

The answer is simple: he did not. The first giveaway about that is the bullet item immediately below the underlined phrase: 'The Governing body is headed by Minister for Women and Child Development.' Why would a government minister head an organization whose funding the government itself finds suspicious?

The answer to that is simpler. This is actually a government scheme.

No great feat of investigative journalism led me to that conclusion. I simply typed '*Traditionally, women in Chhattisgarh have a comparatively higher*' into my nearest Google search box and clicked through to the first result of that search. You can do the same.

The identical document – I mean *identical*, down to the fonts it uses – appears on the Chhattisgarh government's *official website*.[32]

When you visit the home page on that site, the label on your browser window reads: 'Official website Govt. of Chhattisgarh - Profile, Vision, Schemes, Statistics, Resources, Industries, Tourism, History, Whoswho'. One of those government schemes is *Mahila Kosh*. It is headed by one of the government's own ministers, and its initial corpus of Rs 1 crore was set up by the government of Chhattisgarh itself.

Yet, in something straight out of *1984*, or Kafka, the same government of Chhattisgarh turns this on its head. It uses its own scheme, its own Rs 1 crore corpus, as evidence against Sen. To put questions in your mind about Sen.

The Cop

Consider one last document printed off Sen's computer.

On the contents page, the entry reads: 'Appeal from the National President (PUCL), People War Group, Maoist Community (*sic*) Centre, Naxalite, POTA-Like Laws.' It lists these scary names without any comment. My guess is that the entry seeks to put a spectre of Sen's connections with all these nasty people into your brain. What kind of appeal is this anyway?

On 'Chhattisgarh Lok Swatantrya Sangathan (PUCL)' letterhead, this is the document the entry refers to:

> Appeal from the National President of PUCL
> The National President of the People's Union for Civil Liberties (PUCL), Shri K.G. Kannabiran has appealed for the unconditional released (*sic*) of Shri Prakash Soni Sub-Inspector of police, who was recently abducted from Kunakonda block, reportedly by activist (*sic*) of the People's War Group (PWG). In this context it is worthy of special notice that Shri Kannabiran, who is a senior advocate of Hyderabad, has been closely associated at all steps with bringing about the talks between the PWG and the Andhrapradesh (*sic*) Government.
>
> At the same time, the Chhattisgarh PUCL demands that the Government of Chhattisgarh take all steps to initiate unconditional talks with the PWG and the Maoist Communist Centre (MCC). The CRPF should be withdrawn immediately from the so-called Naxalite affected areas. Encounter killings should be halted forthwith and all POTA-like laws withdrawn.
> (Dr Binayak Sen)
> General Secretary
> Chhattisgarh PUCL

In this appeal are the names and phrases that were extracted for the entry in the table of contents, even if 'Maoist Communist Centre' got transformed into 'Maoist Community Centre'.

But what's particularly interesting is the critical detail that the police did not put into the entry in the table: The very first sentence in this Appeal calls, with no ifs and buts, for the '*unconditional release*' of the PSI.

What actually happened with Prakash Soni? I found out, and again, it was no feat of investigative journalism to do so. Google his name and you will learn: after holding him for sixteen days, the PWG released Prakash Soni, unharmed, in October 2004. They did so because the government conceded four of their demands.

So this was no unconditional release as Sen and the PUCL had demanded via this letter. Instead, the Chhattisgarh government capitulated to Maoist demands before he was released.

Yet, bringing to mind Kafka and *1984* again, Sen's explicit call to set this officer free *unconditionally* is turned around to damn Sen. His appeal mentions various Maoist groups, therefore we must infer that he has links with them and assume the attendant opprobrium.

What's more, this effort to tar Sen worked well. In paragraph 96 of his judgement sentencing Sen to life in prison, sessions judge BP Verma observes this and only this about Sen's appeal regarding Prakash Soni: *'People's War Group (PWG) dwara Sub-Inspector Prakash Soni ke apharan ke baat kahi gayi hai'* ('the kidnapping of Sub-Inspector Prakash

Soni by People's War Group (PWG) is mentioned'). He doesn't note that Soni's kidnapping is mentioned only because Sen calls for Soni's unconditional release.

This is necessarily just a sample of what's in that collection of print-outs. They range from banal, like the letter from Pranhita Sen above, to ludicrous, like the mention of the chimpanzee, to perverse and twisted, like the Fernandes note or the Mahila Kosh plan. There is plenty more. Pretty much all the documents can be deconstructed like I have done above. There is nothing remotely incriminating in any of them, unless innuendo and insinuation amounts to incrimination.

Yet were I to pick apart each of the documents, deconstruct each of them, you'd have in your hands a gigantic tome with nothing else in it. And I imagine that's what the prosecution must have known, only too well, about any attempt to counter their efforts. Here's how I imagine their reasoning played out: gather up a large pile of documents, index them so that their meaning is masked behind implication, submit the whole thing to court as 'evidence'. Count on nobody having the patience to peruse each of the documents, the certainty that proper perusal will necessarily produce an unreadable tome and that the implications themselves substitute for actual reading and analysis.

Put it another way: drown the Sen case in paper. Who's going to sift through it all?

But it's only now, after reading and comprehending this pile of paper, that I have an inkling of what's meant by something I referred to earlier, about cases in which law enforcement authorities submit to the courts charge sheets running to thousands of pages. The 2008 bomb blasts in Malegaon, for example, prompted the police to produce a charge sheet that consisted of 4000 pages.[33]

Are several hundred of those 4000 pages something like what's in this chapter?

11

Interlude: So Says the Chart

This chart too, I notice, has curves that snake across it.

Our paediatrician measures our son's height and weight, and plots both on a growth chart. The curves are percentiles, and they tell us the good news: at nine-and-a-half, our son is taller than 97 per cent of kids his age, and heavier than 75 per cent of them.

'Ideally,' says the doc, 'those two numbers should match better.' Because they don't, he is the tall, slender child he is. 'But there's really nothing to worry about,' adds our paediatrician quickly, reassuringly, though I'm not worried at all. The kid is active and healthy, what more could I want? These percentiles interest me little, this mismatch even less.

There are, however, some lines of fine print at the bottom of the chart – which I'll return to. For now, this experience – the chart, the curves, the numbers plotted – reminds me of Joda, just a few years ago. I remember.

Joda is a small iron mining town in Orissa's Keonjhar district. After arrowing inland from the coastal plain, the road that takes us there winds through mute hills and sombre stands of sal trees. Joda sits in a valley like a shallow bowl, surrounded by more hills. Some of them, I realize with a start, are great heaps of slag from the mines. Everything here is in shades of ochre. The roads, the cars and buses, even assorted menacing stands of mining machinery, are coated with the leavings of mining. Yet Joda is not chaotic and grubby, as many Indian small towns are. Where we stay, on a rise above the bowl, the view is dramatic, the air is crisp and flowers abound. Looking up at Orion in a brilliant night sky, I can believe this is one of the country's fabled hill stations, destination for hordes of honeymooners.

Which it isn't, of course. The people milling about on Joda's streets, they are not honeymooning. They are migrant tribals who come to work in the mines – men and women alike, at jobs ranging from digging out the ore to filling railway wagons with it. At the time we visit, this hard labour earns them about Rs 2000 per month. Nowhere else in this area, in Orissa or the neighbouring states, are they paid as much.

Most of the mine workers live in Banspani, a colony of mostly mud huts on the edge of town. One morning there, I visit a daycare centre (an *anganwadi*) a local organization runs for the workers' children. About two dozen bright-eyed, cheerful and skinny kids play and sing around me as I pore over a sheaf of charts and weight records for a child's first five years. The government of Orissa prints and distributes these charts, and requires daycare centres to fill them in. There's one for each kid who has ever passed through the centre, maybe a hundred in all. It's meticulously recorded data, and it tells some thought-provoking tales.

First, every single kid recorded in this sheaf was malnourished, most seriously. The chubbiest on record was 13 kg at five years old. At that age, my son weighed 21 kg.

Second, most children were actually normal at birth. Yet, by six months of age, every single child had sunk into malnutrition, there to stay. Padmabati, the woman in charge, had a one-English-word explanation for this: 'Neglect'. Pressured to work and earn, both parents leave home for long hours, neglecting their children almost from birth. 'Mothers don't breastfeed,' said Padmabati. 'Other kids who are only slightly older look after their little brothers and sisters and bring them here.'

Third, the charts showed frequent sharp weight losses from one month to the next, courtesy bouts of diarrhoea or malaria. In already malnourished children, such attacks are devastating. Sometimes, going by plots that end abruptly, they are fatal.

Fourth, the charts had curves marked on them. Labelled '1', '2', '3' and '4', they represent four grades of malnutrition: '1' goes from 2.75 kg at birth to 15 at 5 years. '4', from 1.5 to 9. '2' and '3' lie in between.

Four grades of malnutrition, actually preprinted on these sheets. The government of Orissa presumes that kids of migrant tribal workers will be malnourished, and so it preprints. And in fact the government is wise to presume, because every child here is indeed malnourished. In fact, most hover between grades '3' and '4', and several have spent spells chugging along below '4'.

Four curves in Banspani that narrate a story about my country.

In 2003, N.C. Saxena, a respected ex-bureaucrat, told that story to the Supreme Court. As part of its deliberations in a PUCL petition about the right to food, the Court asked Saxena to survey hunger across the country. (His travels to gather material took him through this part of Orissa as well.) In his report[34], Saxena observed: '*India remains one of the most undernourished countries in the world, with about half of all children suffering from undernutrition.*' Not much has changed since. The International Food Policy Research Institute describes Indian hunger levels as 'alarming'[35]. Their annual Global Hunger Index regularly ranks us among the world's most malnourished countries, outdone only by such hungrier nations as Mali, Eritrea and Sierra Leone.

If that's dismal, it may get worse. The doctor with whom I visited Joda tells me that if we returned there today, we'd see higher levels of malnutrition. From the rural clinic where she later worked, she once sent me some Government of India data on nutrition levels, with this comment: 'You can see that the proportion of children wasted (indicating acute hunger) has increased.' ('Wasted' means abnormally thin for their height.) A colleague of hers reminded me simply: 'Malnourishment is just a medically sanitized term for hunger.' Sanitized or not, they think it's on the rise. The data apart, at their clinic they're seeing a steady increase in TB cases, always good indicators of chronic and acute hunger.

Back in our pediatrician's chamber, his chart tells altogether another kind of story about the country. It too has preprinted curves, though these are not malnutrition grades. They are labelled simply as percentiles. Still, the five percentile line on his chart nicely matches the grade '1' line from Joda, meaning that five per cent of the children who use his chart will be at or below Orissa's least serious level of malnutrition. (95 per cent, then, are above.)

Yet, according to those Joda charts most children there – I would say over ninety of the hundred or so that I examined – were malnourished to a degree far worse than grade '1'. So much worse, that it would make no sense to use my pediatrician's chart for those kids. Their height-weight plots would creep along the bottom of the grid.

Why does this happen? And what children are we talking about anyway?

The answers appear in those lines I mentioned far above, at the bottom of the chart from our pediatrician. The percentile curves, says the fine print, are adapted from a 1994 paper in the journal *Indian Pediatrics*.[36] The introduction says:

> 'The objective of the present study was to investigate the growth performance of Indian children below six years of age, not subject to any obvious socio-economic constraints that could be expected to impair growth, [and thus] only children [from] affluent population segments ... were selected.'

There is no way, then, to have meaningful growth charts that apply to all Indian kids. They have to be different, based on whether the children are from 'affluent' families or from migrant mining families. That's a story about India.

12

Judgement

Question: What's more alarming than a prosecution that relies on insinuation and twisting?

Answer: a judgement that doesn't just allow such insinuation and twisting to happen and stand, but actually seems to rely on it in coming to a verdict. This is the tragedy of Sen's case. For all we hear about the judiciary being the bulwark of democracy, Sen's experience doesn't inspire much confidence in that bulwark. If this is how we nurture and protect hard-won ideas of freedom and justice, we should all be worried.

But don't take my word for it. Read the judgement for yourself, react to it as any ordinary Indian citizen would, and assess how you feel[37]. It's what I did. I didn't even get near various legal and technical niceties in the judgement – for example, that police officers did not observe provisions of the Indian Evidence Act, or that there are contradictions between separate police accounts of the same arrest, or that Sen's defence contests the claim that a particular piece of evidence was found in his home.

I just read it.

Unlawful Activities and Codes

In Paragraph 4, the judge sets out the 'narrative of the prosecution' ('*abhiyojan ka mamla*'). He starts with an account of Piyush Guha's arrest, which goes something like this: one day the police in Raipur received a tip about the possible movements of Maoists in the area. At some point that same day, Guha walked towards the railway station in Raipur to catch a train. A police team stopped him and searched his bag. In it, they found 'a lot of Naxalite literature and books and booklets'. Also, three handwritten letters which 'had been written to inspire terrorist, Naxalite activities.' Also, Rs 49,000.

Whatever you might think of these finds, what do you make of the next sentence in Paragraph 4? 'Finding the accused involved in 'Naxalite and terrorist activities and unlawful activities against the government, etc.', accused Piyush Guha was taken into custody.'

The handwritten letters the judge refers to are, as you probably guessed, the ones Narayan Sanyal is supposed to have given to Binayak Sen, quoted in full earlier in this book. The judge observes that Sen then gave them to Guha 'in order to send them to the secret code numbers listed in these letters.' (The original Hindi reads like this: '... *patron mein ankit gopaniya code numberon par preshit kiye jane hetu pradatt kiya gaya tha.*')

If you've read this far in this book, you've read those letters. There are no code numbers, secret or not, in them.

Destructive Activities and Handwaving

Move on to Paragraph 5. It lists for us what the police found when they searched Sen's home: a postcard, a letter addressing Sen as 'comrade', eight CDs, another letter, a booklet, etc. The judge writes that while investigating this material, the prosecution found that –

> the accused Narayan Sanyal, who was lodged in jail, and who is a member of the highest organization of the Naxalites-Maoists, the 'Politburo', executed destructive activities of the Naxalites with the help of accused Binayak Sen and Piyush Guha, which were found to amount to 'sedition.'

Sedition is one of the most serious offenses in Indian law and these men are being tried for committing it, yet all we are told about what they actually did are the two words 'destructive activities'.

Besides, there is also the Supreme Court's famous articulation of what constitutes sedition, in *Kedarnath* vs *State of Bihar*: absent a direct incitement to violence, it cannot be sedition. Since *Kedarnath* dates from 1962[38], and is widely known in legal circles, I assume the prosecution knows about this articulation. So was there a direct incitement to violence in the material the police found in Sen's home? If so, what was it?

Paragraph 43 is a model of succinct reasoning, and I will quote it (in translation) in full:

> As far as accused Dr Binayak Sen's involvement in Naxalite activities is concerned, prosecution witness Anil Kumar in section 3 of his statement said that accused Piyush Guha, on being questioned about where he had acquired the documents seized from him, replied that Binayak Sen used to go to meet with Narayan Sanyal in jail and that that was how the said letters were given to Dr Binayak Sen.

Let me recount how Anil Kumar shows up in this prosecution, as laid out in the judgement. When the police stopped Piyush Guha on his way to the Raipur station, they wanted to question him, then search him and his bags. To make such an operation legal, they needed witnesses. Paragraph 14 tells us what happened:

> A team of police constables was sent to call nearby people so that [Guha] could be questioned in their presence, but nearby people did not come. Upon this, people walking on the street were stopped, who were Anil Kumar Singh and Rajesh Gupta.

Paragraph 15 repeats this from Anil Kumar's point of view: 'One day when he was going to the railway station in front of Samrat Talkies, he saw policemen waving their hands and he stopped.'

This Anil Kumar witnessed the police questioning Guha. He made a statement that mentions one answer Guha gave. The prosecution repeated this for the court. This third-hand recounting of Guha's answer, according to Paragraph 43, demonstrates 'Sen's involvement in Naxalite activities'.

Discovered Documents and Globing

Paragraph 45 repeats, in a little more detail, the list of documents the police found while searching Sen's house. Here they are:

> A small yellow book regarding merger between the Communist Party of India Marxist People's War and the Indian Maoist Communist MCCI, Peoples March special issue of November-December 2004, a total of 16 pages, one letter from Madan Lal Barkade, addressed to 'Comrade Binayak Sen,' one English note on Andhra Pradesh Human Rights and Naxalite groups in 3 pages, one photocopy of a 4-page handwritten note in English, in which world globing of republic of present state and other important things were written, Krantikari Janwadi Morcha (RDF), globalisation and Indian service sector's flourishing, total of 8 pages, one post

card which was addressed to accused Binayak Sen, in which the sender's name was Narayan Sanyal; total of 10 paper cuttings, and one Salwa Judum book.

This list begs a number of questions, and rather loudly at that. Is merely possessing this material a crime? Is being addressed as 'comrade' a crime? What is 'important' about the phrase 'world globing of republic of present state' (the judgement actually spells this phrase out in Devanagari) and what does it mean, anyway? Also, what are the 'other important things' that were written in that note?

About Relatives

Later in the judgement, several paragraphs deal with the issue of Sen's visits to the Raipur jail to meet Narayan Sanyal. The prosecution claims that in some of these visits, Sen 'claimed' to be a 'relative' of Sanyal. Paragraph 54 sees the first mention of this claim: 'On 22.7.2006 Dr Binayak Sen claiming to be a relative, met with prisoner Narayan Sanyal to discuss domestic matters.'

Now every time Sen visited Sanyal in jail, he formally wrote a letter to the authorities asking for permission to do so. During the trial, Sen's wife Ilina filed an RTI application asking for copies of these letters. She received them, and so found that on Chhattisgarh PUCL letterhead, on 22 July 2006, Sen had written this letter:

Dear Sir,
Please allow me to meet Shri Narayan Sanyal, who is an undertrial in your jail.
Thank you.
Yours faithfully,
[sd] Binayak Sen

There is no mention that Sen is related to Sanyal. In fact, there is no such mention in any of the letters Sen wrote seeking permission to visit Sanyal. Yet in Paragraph 55, detailing the testimony of jailor S.R. Thakur, a prosecution witness, the claim is repeated about several more dates.

Yet Paragraph 55 ends by observing that 'in his cross-examination, [witness Thakur] acknowledged that in applications submitted by accused Dr Binayak Sen for meetings with accused Narayan Sanyal, he did *not* write saying that he was his relative.' [Emphasis added]

So did Sen make this claim of being Sanyal's relative or not? More pertinently, what did the court make of this allegation by the prosecution?

That's answered in Paragraph 58:

> Although, the accused during the examination of the accused have denied that the pretext of 'relative' was used for the meetings, but since the testimony of the witnesses has been unchallenged, it is established that accused Binayak Sen met with Narayan Sanyal on the various dates cited above by claiming to be his relative.

Sen denies that he claimed to be Sanyal's relative. But more than that, the judge himself records (remember Paragraph 55) that at least one witness who made this claim – Thakur the jailor – admitted under cross-examination that Sen did in fact *not* claim to be Sanyal's relative. How did the judge conclude that 'the testimony of the witnesses has been unchallenged'? – when Sen himself challenged this claim, when the witness himself changed his mind? How did the judge conclude that Sen did indeed claim to be Sanyal's relative when Sen specifically denied it and when this witness specifically denied it?

Sitting with Sen in Raipur some days after he was released on bail in April 2011, I asked him about being Sanyal's relative. He explained that the jail register was maintained by another prisoner. For every visitor to the jail, this prisoner would fill in the names of prisoner and visitor. To describe the relationship between them, this prisoner routinely entered 'relative'. Nobody paid it much attention. Even a cursory look at the register, Sen said, would show that the word is in that prisoner's handwriting.

Why would a prosecution and a judge not take note of this and ascribe it to a bored prisoner's routine scribbling? Why would they not match it with Sen's letters asking for permission to visit – not one of which mentions him being Sanyal's relative – and conclude what any reasonable observer of all this would conclude? Is it conceivable that Sen would not mention 'relative' while seeking permission to visit, but mention it in a different hand in the jail register?

Is it conceivable that he would do this not once or twice, but – as the buzz about the case has it – *thirty-three* times?

Rupantar and its Registration

The Sens established Rupantar formally in the early 1990s, specifically to work with people who, according to one of its brochures, 'have been marginalized in the formal process of development'. For example, Rupantar has put together teaching materials in Chhattisgarhi for tribals and slum dwellers in Raipur. They have trained and placed community health workers (known locally as *mitanin*) in a number of villages in the district. These workers are able to address a number of basic health issues, like TB, malaria, diarrhoea and respiratory infections. Rupantar has also focused on measures to help tribal farmers to improve their production, by promoting 'locally sustainable' seeds and alternate crops.

These brief details, incidentally, are chosen from documents the Chhattisgarh police took from the Sens' computer and used to pursue their case against Sen. In that pursuit, both the police and prosecution have made several accusations about Rupantar, and it's worth examining them in some detail.

Paragraph 91 in the judgement, for example, makes a connection between the Sens and the Naxalites: 'Rupantar is an organization of Naxalites in Raipur, which is run by Ilina Sen and accused Dr Binayak Sen.'

Paragraph 96 tells us that one of the documents about Rupantar speaks of a workshop that was to happen on 7–8 January 2004. The Sens were going to be present, as also was 'Shankar (who is a hardcore Naxalite and is currently absconding)'. Also notable about this document, according to this paragraph, is that 'the word 'comrade', used for addressing Naxalites, is mentioned.'

Mention of 'comrade' apart, what was this workshop? It was a 'Consultation in Chhattisgarh on National Police for Women's Empowerment'. Among the attendees listed are Asha Shukla, Assistant Editor of *Navbharat*, Raipur; Dr Jayashree Kurup, Director of the Student Service Centre at IGNOU; Dr Indira Mishra, Additional Chief Secretary of Chhattisgarh (who also served as principal secretary in various government departments in Madhya Pradesh and Chhattisgarh); and Dr Sudha Malaiya, a BJP leader then in the National Commission on Women and wife of Jayant Malaiya, who, in 2012, was Minister of Housing and Environment in Madhya Pradesh.[39]

If one Shankar's presence at this workshop imputes Naxalism to the Sens and Rupantar, what should we make of the presence at the *same* workshop of Ms Shukla and Drs Kurup, Mishra and Malaiya? What does their presence say about the Sens and Rupantar? Should Shankar's taint apply to these women too?

Referring to another Rupantar document, Paragraph 97 says it mentions 'hardcore Naxalite Amita Srivastava whom the prosecution describes as absconding.'

She may be absconding, but this document is a copy

of an application form for a grant from the Department of Elementary Education and Literacy. In particular, this grant is under the 'Education Guarantee and Alternative Innovative Educational Programme of the Sarva Shiksha Abhiyan – Experimental and Innovative component *funded directly by Government of India*.'[40] [Emphasis added]

This incriminating document is, yes, an application submitted to the government for government funds. I cannot help wondering: at the time it was submitted, did some official scrutinizing it, leap up, shouting, for all to hear, that it mentions the 'hardcore Naxalite Amita Srivastava'?

But moving ahead to Paragraph 111, the narrative shifts into a higher gear. The third sentence in this paragraph says 'Rupantar organization is a registered institution which is audited'. But having stated this, the paragraph swiftly turns this assertion on his head. Sen's defence, we learn, has produced no documents to show that Rupantar is a 'registered institution', and therefore Rupantar 'does not seem to be [a] government registered organization.' With that, and because Rupantar employed Shankar Singh and Binayak Sen, we learn, it is 'evident that the accused Binayak Sen was involved in Naxalite activities and used to shelter and support these activities'.

How that last inference holds is debatable, rather than 'evident'. But let's go back for a moment to the document referred to in Paragraph 97, the application for a grant on the form from the Department of Elementary Education and Literacy. On the first page of this application form – indeed, it's the *very first* entry on the form – you will find this: 'Name of Organization: Rupantar (A Public Charitable Trust) Registration (Under Trust Act) No. 8693 on 17.11.94 at Delhi.'

The very document in which the prosecution notices mention of an absconding Naxalite also mentions Rupantar's registration details. Even with this, the prosecution claims that Rupantar is *not* registered.

The prosecution and the judge actually do this a second time. Right after the mention of Amita Srivastava – in the same sentence, in fact – Shankar makes another appearance. In a second document presented to court, says the judgement, 'Shankar Singh, who also is claimed by the prosecution to be a hardcore Naxalite, is shown as an employee of Rupantar organization.'

Three things to note about this other document:

One, it is a 'Pre Grant Application Form For Potential NGO Partner', to be submitted to a New Delhi organization called REACH India.

Two, there is no mention of 'Shankar Singh' in this document. A 'Shankar' is indeed 'shown as an employee of Rupantar' there, but there's no 'Singh' attached to that name. Apart from the validity of imputing guilt to Rupantar merely because its grant application lists someone the prosecution calls a 'hardcore Naxalite', we don't even know for certain that this person is the 'hardcore Naxalite' in question.

Three, on the first page of this application form too, you will find this: 'Registration no 8693 Date: 17.11.94'. (Also 'FCRA No: 231650876, Year 1998')

Once more, the very document which the prosecution

and judge use to show that Rupantar employs a 'hardcore Naxalite' also states Rupantar's registration details.

The Muslims

If all this is strange enough, return once more to Paragraph 97 for the jewel that's sewn into this fabric of insinuation, via a few more references to documents found on Sen's computer (including the one above that refers to Amita Srivastava). The judge writes:

> 'There is a message about the death of Pakistan's Omar Asghar Khan and [elsewhere] Maher Arak has been written about. In this way ... the names of Yasin Malik and Ghulam Rasool Dhar of the Jammu Kashmir Liberation Front have been mentioned.'
> (*Pakistan ke Omar Asghar Khan ki mrityu ka sandesh hai tatha ... Maher Arak ke bare mein likha hai. ... Jammu Kashmir Liberation Front ke Yasin Malik va Ghulam Rasool Dhar ke naam ka ullekh hai.*)

Four names in one paragraph; in fact, in two successive sentences. What do we know about each of them?

First, Omar Asghar Khan[41]. The 'message about the death' of this man is an email note that the late writer/activist Smitu Kothari sent out to a number of friends. Kothari's email, in full:

Dear friends,
It is with deep sadness and shock that I would like to share the news of the sudden death of a very dear Pakistani friend, Omar Asghar Khan.
Smitu
Achin, Could you paste this to the Coalition and to our MIND list?
Smitu Kothari
Research Director, Lokayan
13, Alipur Road, Delhi 110054

Kothari wrote this note and sent it out to a number of people, Sen being one of them. What could the prosecution and the judge have had against this?

Next, Maher Arak. Arak is a Canadian of Syrian descent. The document the judge refers to is his statement 'This is What They Did To Me'[42], which was widely circulated by email a few years ago. Again, it made its way to Sen's computer by email, from where the police selected it and used it to buttress the prosecution of Sen.

In 2002, Arak was wrongly arrested in the US, deported to Syria and tortured there. The details are not relevant here; but note that Syria's government later declared him 'completely innocent'.[43] The Canadian government 'publicly cleared [him] of any links to terrorism' and awarded him a $10.5 million settlement; in 2007, that country's prime minister, Stephen Harper, personally apologized to Arak.[44]

Again, you have to ask: why is any of this of any relevance to Sen's guilt or otherwise?

Finally, Yasin Malik and Ghulam Rasool Dhar: both are indeed members of the JKLF. Their names figure in a document the judgement mentions, again taken from Sen's computer. It is part of the printed schedule of the World Social Forum, held in Bombay in January 2004, because both men appeared and spoke at the WSF.

The question, yet again: so what? What about the death of a random Pakistani man does the prosecution find objectionable? What about an account by a Canadian of his arrest, torture and later exoneration does it find objectionable? What about the mention of two Kashmiris in the WSF schedule does it find objectionable?

And there's a more troubling question to answer as well: why do these four names appear in two successive sentences in this judgement?

Is it because they are all Muslim names? Is that the only thing that ties them together, the only thing about them that raises suspicion? Is it now a crime to keep in your inbox email messages that mention Muslims?

Unity of Minds on Sedition

As you can imagine, like with other prosecution documents in this case, there is plenty to be said about this judgement. Naturally I've only touched on some of it here.

But there is one final pronouncement that deserves thought and attention, and it appears in Paragraph 112.

Here are two sentences from that paragraph:

It has been found in the investigation above that the [three letters] were written by the accused Narayan Sanyal in Central Jail, Raipur which were given to the accused Dr Binayak Sen during their meeting in the jail, and those letters were further given to the accused Piyush Guha with the aim of sending them to various Naxalite organisations etc addressed to some code names. This proves the facts of unity of minds of the accused and criminal conspiracy of sedition against the State.

(*Upar vivechana mein yeh paya ja chuka hai ki Article A-8 se A-10 ka patra abhiyukt Narayan Sanyal dvara Kendriya Jail Raipur mein likha gaya, jise jail mein mulakat ke darmayaan abhiyukt Dr Binayak Sen ko pradhan kiye gaye tatha ukta patron ko vibhinna Naxali sanghathanon/sangamon ityadi mein code words ke naam se bhejne hetu abhiyukt Piyush Gupta ko pradhan kiya gaya. Jisse abhiyuktagun ke mastishk ki ekta ('Unity of Mind') evam rajdroh karne ka aapradhik shadyantra kiye jaane ke tathya pramanit hote hain.*)

Even if the prosecution did establish this chain of handing over letters – which is itself contested – the prime question about this episode remains to be asked again: how does this even suggest, let alone 'prove', sedition?

13

Interlude: Prisoners

What do you say to the citizen who needs only to hear words like 'Naxalite' or 'Maoist' to believe everything a government says, suspending otherwise admirably alert faculties of scepticism about how governments work? Then there are those who confess to 'loathing' Sen and being sure he is guilty. Why? Because 'he's a Naxalite', or because 'he met that Maoist Sanyal in jail'.

But why does meeting a prisoner induce loathing? Also, how much do we know about people who occupy our jails?

Some years ago, I was arrested, along with some 60 others, for travelling in the ladies' first-class compartment of a Bombay suburban train. There's nothing convincing to say in my defence, so I won't try.

At the police station, we were given two choices: spend the night in jail, or pay Rs 500 as bail and go home. In both cases, we had to appear in court the next day to pay our fines. A nearby guardian angel was able to bail me out; but when I left, not one of my partners in crime looked likely to go free that night. Whatever they decided, I looked forward to renewing my friendships with them in court.

The next day, I was the only one in court. While waiting for the judge, a clerk beckoned me forward. 'You shouldn't have come here!' he whispered. 'You should have just warmed the cops' hands!' ('*Unka haath garam karna tha!*' – the old euphemism for paying a bribe.) 'The others did that and went home last night.'

Yet my most vivid memories of that day are of prisoners. While I waited, the police brought in streams of prisoners for hearings. All male, mostly young, bedraggled, frightened and bewildered prisoners. All roped together in a long line, they shuffled in under barked orders from accompanying constables, who then pushed them down on the floor. There they squatted, like a line of captive circus bears.

This is how the next hour or so went.

The judge would call out a name: 'Swapnil Gajbhiye!'

Prodded by a constable, one of the boys would rise from his squat, rope trailing down to his compatriots ahead and behind him. Head bowed, he'd stand and wait. Judge and clerk would confabulate with each other for a short while, looking repeatedly at a calendar. Finally the judge would look at the boy and announce a date sometime in the future. Pushed by the constable again, the hapless prisoner would squat, and the judge moved on to the next name.

There was no method to this crazy procedure. The dates were all over the calendar – 7 March, 15 February, 26 April

– though all within the next three months. These were the dates for the next 'hearing' in each case. What would happen in that next hearing? Likely another date picked for another future hearing.

I have no idea what happened to those boys. Did they get bail? Were they ever sentenced and if so, have they served their sentences? Was there any chance their sentences were offset against time they had already served in custody? Were they able to appeal their sentences to higher courts, perhaps all the way up to the Supreme Court? Did the Supreme Court see fit to make observations about their cases, as it did in the case of Sen?

For every minutely followed Binayak Sen – about whose case even books get written – there must be hundreds who don't see the light of justice and who must battle not just a system deaf to their plight, but a wall of public indifference. Historian Ramachandra Guha wrote of concerns similar to these, when he visited a jail in Jagdalpur, Chhattisgarh. At the time, the jail housed 1337 prisoners, and Guha met one of them:

> 'I had a conversation with a prisoner named Dabba Boomaiah. He was a soft-spoken Muria in his twenties, from a village named Bamanpur near Bhopalpatnam. He told me the story of how he now found himself in Jagdalpur jail. He had, he said, a job as a labourer on a lift irrigation project. One day, at work, he was passed by a road-building crew, who asked him the way to Bhopalpatnam police station. He escorted them

there, but was then detained by the police. They began quizzing him about the presence of Naxalites in his village. Then they asked him to join the Salwa Judum. He said he couldn't become a vigilante, since he had a wife, two small kids and a widowed mother to support. Thereupon they arrested him.

It was now three months since Dabba Boomaiah took the road-building crew to Bhopalpatnam police station. After his arrest, he had been taken to Dantewada jail, from where he was shifted to Jagdalpur. He had not seen his wife and children since his arrest. When I asked why he hadn't been in touch with his family, he answered that they had never even visited Dantewada town. How then could they come to Jagdalpur, which was many hours away? However, he was in touch with a lawyer, who would represent him in a court hearing, which was scheduled for the following week. At that hearing, Dabba Boomaiah hoped to get bail, and be permitted to rejoin the family.

I do not know whether Dabba Boomaiah got bail, whether the charges against him were dropped, whether he is still in Jagdalpur prison or has been reunited with his wife and children. A friend who knows the region well tells me that hearings are often cancelled at the last minute, as the criminal court in Jagdalpur is short of staff. Besides, cases against alleged Naxalites demand extra security, and when this is not available the cases are postponed.

... In the eyes of the Raipur sessions court, Sen's

'crime' was that he had talked to Maoist prisoners and was alleged to have Maoist literature in his home. The guilt they presumed was by association and insinuation, for Sen was not himself a member of the Maoist party, nor had he committed acts of violence or otherwise broken the law. Association and insinuation had also landed Dabba Boomaiah in jail. His 'crime' was that he happened to live in a district that had seen intense Maoist activity, and where a suspicious and paranoid state government demanded that everyone take sides.

From what one hears and knows, there are thousands of Dabba Boomaiahs languishing in the jails of Andhra Pradesh, Maharashtra, Jharkhand, Chhattisgarh and Orissa, thousands of adivasis innocent of all crimes except that of having made their home in districts where insurgents and the police are ranged against one another. *Pace* the Supreme Court judgment, these adivasis have not read Mao; indeed, have not even heard of Mao. But they live in areas where Maoists are active and influential; which makes them, in the eyes of what passes for the law in these tragic, troubled parts of India, Maoists themselves.

When the judge in Raipur sentenced Binayak Sen to life imprisonment, the home minister said that he could always appeal to a higher court. Most victims of the civil war in Chhattisgarh, however, do not have such recourse. They are at the mercy of an arbitrary and often brutal police, and of lower courts shot through with corruption and subject to intimidation.

For someone like Dabba Boomaiah, New Delhi is even more distant than Jagdalpur is to his family. The Supreme Court deserves three cheers for the relief it has granted Binayak Sen, but pending the suffering of the ordinary adivasi in Maoist-infested areas, let us not raise three cheers for Indian democracy itself.'[45]

Going by what happened to Sen, or to Dabba Boomaiah, anyone who has inadvertent conversations with Maoists might find themselves in jail. Does that in itself make them Maoist?

14

Sedition

Earlier in this book, I briefly examined the charge of sedition that was made against Sen, Guha and Sanyal. Here's how Justice B.P. Verma set the stage for his own examination of the charge:

> 'The charges against the accused under [various sections of the IPC, CSPSA and UAPA] are that on or before or around the date of 06.05.2007, on Station Road, Raipur (Chhattisgarh), in Central Jail Raipur (Chhattisgarh) or Central Jail Bilaspur (Chhattisgarh) or Katora Talab Raipur (Chhattisgarh) or Hotel Mahendra Raipur or Hotel Gitanjali Raipur, they conspired to wage war, or conspired to an attempt to wage such war or conspired to abet such war against the Indian state or the state government, and by words, either spoken or written, or by signs, or by visible representation, or otherwise,

> brought or attempted to bring into hatred or contempt, or excited or attempted to excite disaffection towards the Government established by law in India, and thus committed sedition or conspired to commit sedition.'

When Justice Verma had heard and seen all the evidence presented to support this charge, he observed:

> 'During investigation, it was found that the accused Narayan Sanyal, who was lodged in jail, and who is a member of the highest organization of the Naxalites-Maoists, the Politburo', executed destructive activities of the Naxalites with the help of accused Binayak Sen and Piyush Guha, which were found to amount to sedition.'

Later in his judgement, Justice Verma explains that Sanyal gave three letters to Sen, and Sen gave these letters to Guha –

> '... with the aim of sending them to various Naxalite organizations. This proves the facts of unity of minds of the accused and criminal conspiracy of sedition against the State.'

And later still, immediately before pronouncing his sentence:

> 'Accused persons have committed the serious crime of the criminal conspiracy of sedition against a lawfully established government in India.'

The judge used the sedition charge, as laid out here, to sentence three Indian citizens to life in prison. For that reason alone, this case offers a chance to explore the implications of sedition and what it means to accuse someone of it.

The word itself triggers strong feelings, no different from words like treason and traitor. This is only natural. We are all conditioned to strong feelings about the country we live in, taught from an early age that patriotism is the highest virtue there is. Correspondingly, we learn that being a traitor, or being seditious, is the greatest of crimes. These are 'hot-button' words that when used, set off revulsion that leaves no place for argument and reason.

For examples of this, check the comments that articles about Binayak Sen generate, either on the web, or as letters to newspapers. A report that the Government had asked Sen to join the Planning Commission's steering committee on health[46] generated this reaction (among several others): 'A corrupt government headed by a puppet and remote controlled by an Italian calls a traitor to plan healthcare for the people of this country.' At a public meeting he was invited to in Bombay, several dozen protestors shouted slogans and wanted to know if the organizers were also going to invite Ajmal Kasab, the murderer from 26/11.

That Sen inspires such venom is what the accusation of sedition has accomplished.

But first, let's look at the charge itself. Earlier, I mentioned the 1962 *Kedarnath* case. The Supreme Court ruled there that a prosecution cannot sustain a charge of sedition if the accused did not directly incite violence. Thus we have a test of a charge of sedition against someone: did this person incite violence? If the answer is 'no', there's no case for sedition.

That apart, the word saw plenty of airplay as we moved into the second decade of the twenty-first century: in the debate about Sen's case, but also because of statements from the writer Arundhati Roy. For example, she made a speech at a conference in Delhi on 25 October 2010. She said plenty of things in that speech that were meant to provoke thought and debate, certainly angry thought and debate. But one thing she said, in particular, had people thinking 'sedition'.

One news report put it this way: 'There is a growing debate about ... whether [Roy's] remark that 'Kashmir has never been an integral part of India' bordered on sedition.'[47]

I am uninterested in defending Roy, least of all in a book about Binayak Sen, and in any case she does an excellent job of defending herself. But it's worth considering that remark, as dispassionately as it is possible to be with anything to do with Kashmir, to better understand the meaning of sedition.

To me, the first question to ask is, is it possible to honestly claim that all of Kashmir has been under Indian control since 1947? The answer is no, because Pakistan has held a large section of the state for pretty much all those six-plus decades. Our Indian admission that this is so is implicit and evident in the very name we use for that portion of Kashmir: Pakistan-Occupied Kashmir (POK). We can wave the legal instrument by which Kashmir acceded to India all we want – and that legal accession did in fact happen – but what also did happen, a reality we don't even deny, is the fact of POK.

In what real sense, then, is POK an 'integral part of India'? What is the difference between saying 'Kashmir has never been an integral part of India', and referring to a whole section of that state as 'Pakistan-*Occupied* Kashmir' (emphasis added) for nearly all of our independent history? None. Yet we all say 'POK' without a thought, but Roy's statement might 'border on sedition'.

The second question to ask is, can Roy be allowed to make such a statement? It inflames and offends many people, but can she actually say such a thing? Yes she can, because the Indian Constitution guarantees her the freedom of speech to say anything she wants to say. There are consequences she might have to face, and what she says might offend others, but nothing can stop her from saying what she wants to stay. This is fundamental to the idea of freedom of speech.

The third question to ask is, did what she say amount to sedition? Well, apply the *Kedarnath* test. In saying the words she did, did she directly incite violence among her listeners? Meaning, did she suggest that they go out and burn down a bus, or attack fellow citizens or anything like that? If not, and absent a direct incitement to violence, this cannot be sedition. No doubt some people may have been angered enough by her words to get into scuffles with others around them, but did she diretly incite even that violence?

Clearly not.

In much the same way, it's hard to imagine that even Sen's most virulent critics see his alleged crimes, *as spelled out by Justice Verma*, as an incitement to violence. (Does the delivery of three letters qualify?) If that's so, considering legal precedent alone, the charge of sedition against Sen cannot stand. So where does that leave the prosecution, at least on this charge? *Kedarnath* should have, by itself, been a death blow for Sen's prosecution: what happens, after all, to a case stripped of its most serious charge?

And yet it wasn't the death blow. The case carried on to its end, till Sen was convicted. My suspicion is that this has to do, at least in part, with a general ignorance about what goes on in our judicial system. Precedents don't count for much with people to whom 'sedition' is in fact a hot button.

But because *Kedarnath* is not well known outside legal circles, many of us are quick to demand punishment for people like Sen, who say things we don't like hearing about our country. And a prosecution can get away with simply making the charge of sedition.

This is not to say that Justice Verma did not know about *Kedarnath*. But it is easy for a prosecution to ignore *Kedarnath* in a climate where it matters little to people, where there is instead outrage to capitalize on.

What *Kedarnath* and Sen's case can do – what they should have done – is stimulate a public debate on sedition itself. What constitutes sedition, can it be definitively defined, should it be an offence at all, how should it be punished?

What constitutes sedition? According to Justice Verma, you have committed it if you 'brought or attempted to bring into hatred or contempt, or excited or attempted to excite disaffection towards the government established by law in India.' This is a vast brush. At any given time, plenty of us are dissatisfied with our governments, whether the one in Delhi or those in our state capitals. This has been an Indian truism for decades. But it is especially true in recent years, with the immense public disgust with scams and corruption. Take Anna Hazare and his colleagues and his entire India Against Corruption movement, or the opposition in the Lok Sabha that has spoken loudly about the 2G scam. Are these people not exciting disaffection – as they should, as should we all – towards the government?

But let's make this less abstract and look at something real. A writer I know wrote these words in a July 2011 column:

> 'This government is unwavering in its commitment to corruption of every form [with] its adherence to falsehoods, prevarication and sheer bloody mindedness.'[48]

This is hardly unusual: similar commentaries appear in print and cyberspace all the time. This writer certainly sounds contemptuous of his lawfully established government: it is in fact how he wants to sound. He *wants* to 'excite disaffection towards the government.' So has this writer committed sedition? Can he be charged with it?

The point about defining sedition like this is that it makes criticism of the government an offence. In a democracy, this is meaningless.

When an electorate tires of a government and votes for a change, it is clearly dissatisfied with the government.

When an opposition politician rises in Parliament to criticise the government, he is dissatisfied with it. This is, after all, exactly the way a democracy must function. But electorate and politician alike, they are exciting disaffection. Are they therefore committing sedition?

Yes, you might say, but it's sedition when someone conspires *against the state*. That's different from mere criticism.

Fair enough, but where do you draw the line? Who decides, and how? For example, if someone suggested that promoting free markets is seditious, she'd likely be greeted with laughter and scorn. Yet if you take away the indefensible violence of Maoists for a moment, what Maoists are pursuing is an agenda on the other end of the political spectrum from free market capitalism. At least these days, one of these is perfectably acceptable; the other can get you labelled seditious.

Is ideology a determinant of sedition then? And when societal preferences for ideologies change, as they have throughout history, does sedition find a new definition? In a democracy, again, this is meaningless. If the essence of democracy is that every voice must be heard, some voices will be disagreeable to others. I don't like the demands to build a temple at that spot in Ayodhya; nor the equation of patriotism to singing a particular song; nor the encomiums for unfettered free markets. But in a democracy, we live with opinions we may not like. The holders of those particular opinions are not seditious, nor am I so, merely because we have our views.

Yet even if we ever nail down a leakproof definition of sedition, there remains the question of whether it should be an offence at all. When we have the constitutionally-guaranteed freedom to express ourselves, the idea that some kinds of utterances – but only some – are criminal is perverse. Societies that repress such dissent only destroy themselves. Ask the grey figures who ruled the old Soviet Union for years – Bulganin, Khrushchev, Brezhnev. The price they paid for perpetrating decades of Soviet oppression was the complete collapse of their country.

Yet with Sen, it's not even as if he was accused of saying things unpalatable to the Chhattisgarh government, even though he has done so plenty of times. According to Justice Verma himself, Sen is guilty of 'criminal conspiracy of sedition against the State' because he carried three letters from Narayan Sanyal to Piyush Guha. In fact, if you focus on the language Justice Verma uses, the content of those letters has nothing to do with this criminal conspiracy. According to Justice Verma, Sanyal wrote the letters and gave them to Sen; and then Sen gave them to Guha. In the very next sentence Justice Verma writes in his judgement, 'this proves the facts' of sedition.

Forget *Kedarnath*. Forget incitement to violence. This is sedition based on being a glorified postman.

15

Implications

A right-leaning blogger I know of confessed that, after Binayak Sen was sentenced to life in prison, he (the blogger) was happy because he 'loathed' Sen. They had never met, never spoken, never exchanged letters, but he loathed the man. Why, I asked. 'Because he is a Naxalite', he responded.

The host of questions this exchange raises form, in a real sense, the reason for this book.

Do you pronounce judgement on a man before he has been through the process of justice that he is entitled to? Should you look at, maybe analyse for yourself, the evidence presented in the case against him? Does this evidence really prove that he is a Naxalite, and if so how? Is being a Naxalite, in itself, a crime? Is there a distinction between movement and man?

But of course, we are entitled to our particular loathings.

Therefore the real question to ask is a modified version of something Colin Powell said in 2008. In the face of continuing questions from within his Republican Party about then-candidate Barack Obama's religion and nationality, Powell issued this statement:

> 'I'm also troubled by ... what members of the [Republican] party say. And it is permitted to be said, such things as, 'Well, you know that Mr. Obama is a Muslim.' Well, the correct answer is, he is not a Muslim, he's a Christian. He's always been a Christian. But the really right answer is: What if he is? Is there something wrong with being a Muslim in this country? The answer's no, that's not America. Is there something wrong with some 7-year-old Muslim American kid believing that he or she could be president? Yet I have heard senior members of my own party drop the suggestion, 'He's a Muslim and he might be associated with terrorists.' This is not the way we should be doing it in America.'

What if he is, indeed.

In much the same way, the correct answer to 'Sen is a Naxalite' is that he is not. Not even Naxalites would call Sen one. But the really correct answer is: What if he is? That question informs any understanding of the implications of this case.

Labelling and Scepticism

Call somebody words like 'Naxalite' and 'Maoist', and there's need, apparently, for little more, though telling adjectives often work well. Sen's case has plenty of examples. At several points in the case papers, we see phrases like these:

> Mrs. Amita Shrivastava ... has been working as **hardcore** Naxal commander. [*From the supplementary charge sheet, emphasis added*]
>
> 'While testifying regarding Malati being associated with CPI Maoist [two prosecution witnesses] said that she is a **hardcore** Naxalite.' [*From the December 2010 judgement, emphasis added*]
>
> 'As per prosecution, Shankar Singh Amita Shrivastava are **hardcore** Naxalites.' [*From the February 2011 Chhattisgarh High Court order denying bail to Sen, emphasis added*]

Perhaps for variation, a supplementary charge sheet uses the phrase 'dreaded Naxalite'. That label was for Shoma Sen, whose handwriting was closely examined.

Evidently just pronouncing these people 'hardcore Naxalites' is enough to establish that they are criminals, or at least worthy of suspicion. No need for any additional evidence, nor even an explanation of what's meant by this phrase, nor why it is a crime. The words carry their own halo of guilt. Doesn't everyone find their antennae tingling at the mention of a 'hardcore Naxalite'?

Justice Verma's mention of Malati, cited above, is

sandwiched between one sentence in which the judge says a charge sheet was filed in Raipur against Malati, and another that says she was convicted and sentenced. Thus this is a passage meant to establish her guilt. Yet the sentence I quoted is the *only* mention of what she is guilty of – she is 'associated with CPI Maoist' and somebody says 'she is a hardcore Naxalite.' (If those are crimes.)

In short, Justice Verma has taken note of what the prosecution wanted him to take note of: phrases that raise suspicions.

But why didn't the judge question this? Why didn't he say to the prosecution: 'use whatever labels you want for the accused, but I will make my judgement on the evidence. So if you want me to treat this particular name as an accused, please give me some evidence.'

Maybe these labels actually raise spectres in our minds. But is that proof of guilt?

Yet there's a strange and creeping reluctance to question labelling. If a minister makes pronouncements on education, or cleaning up a city, or fixing potholes in the roads, he will be greeted with snorts of derision. But let him call someone a Maoist, a Naxalite, and we promptly believe him without question. Use a few choice words, and scepticism is tossed out.

I spoke about Sen's case at a meeting once, listing some of my doubts about the case. A man in the audience got up to confront me. 'There can't be smoke without a fire!' he said. 'If the Chief Minister says he's a Maoist, he must be one!' For good measure, he asked: 'Are you a Maoist sympathizer?'

Officials are acutely aware of this power of labels. On 14 April 2011, for example, Chhattisgarh's Home Minister, Nankiram Kanwar, told the press that the doctors of Jan Swasthya Sahyog in Ganiyari have 'Naxal connections.'[49] He knew this, said Kanwar, because these doctors were working to help Sen secure bail.

There were others, remember, who also worked to help Sen secure bail. There were lawyers in Chhattisgarh and New Delhi, innumerable individuals and groups all over India and the world, several Nobel Prize winners and indeed some judges at India's Supreme Court, because the day after Kanwar's pronouncement, the same Supreme Court ordered Sen released on bail. By Kanwar's logic, all these people must have 'Naxal connections.'

Could a Home Minister – the official responsible for a state's law and order – really be this oblivious of the working of the law, the meaning of bail? Why would he say such a thing? But Kanwar knew just what he was doing. His was a label he knew would stick. Plenty of people will now think, without question, that the doctors in Ganiyari have 'Naxal connections.' Kanwar has ensured that.

Health Care

Two rural health care initiatives in Chhattisgarh find mention in this book: the Shaheed Hospital in Dalli-Rajhara, and the Jan Swasthya Sahyog in Ganiyari. There's plenty that's common to both places, but perhaps this most urgently: these days, they are finding it increasingly difficult to recruit new doctors, and especially young doctors, to work for them. When I visited, Dr Saibal Jana at Shaheed Hospital spoke repeatedly of the 'commercialization' of the profession, meaning that doctors today were interested primarily in the chance to make money, and hardly at all in the chance to make a difference to people's lives.

In contrast, here's how Sen's professor of physiology at CMC, the same PZach I mentioned earlier, described Sen's experience in Dalli-Rajhara:

> 'It was a moment of intensive union activity among mine workers. Permanently disenfranchised as casual labourers, these miners were beginning to fight their abysmal conditions, led by the iconic leader Shankar Niyogi. Healthcare was non-existent. Sanitary arrangements were primitive. One of the most active people in their movement died while giving birth. It then became clear to them that the community needed to push for medical care. Binayak set up a clinic with the help of the community that later became the Shaheed Hospital. Miners volunteered and he trained them in nursing, laboratory work, accounts and management. ... Everyone in the hospital, including Binayak, did sanitary work. He empowered them so that they were able to take major policy decisions. They began with ten beds and in the seven years that Binayak was there it became a 90-bed hospital.'[50]

Tot up the themes Zachariah touches on: disenfranchised miners, union activity, non-existent healthcare, primitive sanitation, a death during childbirth, setting up a hospital, miners trained to work in all aspects of running it, building what has become an institution in the area. In the early 1980's, this was the kind of wholesale challenge that health care offered, that Sen and Jana responded to.

Do such challenges exist today? Certainly they do: for example, it's not difficult to visit parts of India where people trudge long distances to find a doctor, parts that could use a hospital. (Bokrakachhar and Bahaud, for example.)

Do doctors respond to such challenges today, as Jana and Sen did in the early 1980s? That's more difficult to answer. I know several doctors who set out on journeys like this and have stayed the course. Yet the worrying reality is that none of them started work more recently than over a decade ago. No wonder Jana and the JSS doctors speak of the difficulty of attracting fresh talent.

Even so, I realize mine is anecdotal evidence. If there are young doctors starting on careers in rural health these days, I'm humbled by their spirit and I'd like to know about them.

One point Zachariah makes is one I've alluded to before: healthcare has connections to the way people live, in every sense. You start off treating cases of TB, and before long you're looking at unions, civil liberties and justice. Perhaps this is the journey Sen made. Seen that way, it is no surprise that he began to annoy people. But is it incumbent on doctors to make connections to these wider concerns? Louis

Lasagna's modern version of the Hippocratic Oath comes close to suggesting as much:

> 'I do not treat a fever chart, a cancerous growth, but a sick human being, whose illness may affect the person's family and economic stability. My responsibility includes these related problems, if I am to care adequately for the sick.'

Most doctors come to know and understand what John Donne said: no man is an island, entire of itself. Doctors do not operate in a vacuum. A patient's condition has repercussions, financial and otherwise, among family and friends. Equally, the situation of the outside world affects the health of a patient. 'Caring adequately for the sick' cannot be an isolated activity.

But if it is not isolated, how far beyond do you go? You could stop with just the immediate family: father, mother, siblings. But then there are cousins. In-laws. The cousins' in-laws. Friends and neighbours. Everybody on the street where a patient lives. His entire village.

And what do you take into account? There's health. But there's also their financial situation. Education. Caste. Access to justice, democracy and governance. How do you draw a line through any of this, or observe one if it does get drawn?

This is the way to think about what rural health care came to mean to Binayak Sen, as it has come to mean to many doctors who work in rural health. So if doctors these days are less interested in working in rural areas, as Jana fears, this means health clinics in rural areas will always be short-staffed. But it also means that less and less doctors – and by extension less and less of us – will make the connections that Sen did; that a general empathy for and understanding of rural India will pass us all by.

The Meaning of Justice

Stripped of rhetoric and a lot of irrelevant documents, the case against Sen comes down to this: he met a Maoist ideologue in jail several times and he carried three letters for this ideologue.

This bare-bones presentation of the case should have by itself alerted the prosecution and the judge – and the rest of us – to its flimsiness. Which of the innumerable sections of the IPC and CrPC is violated here, and how? The prosecution made no case for this. What's in the letters that calls for action by the state against a man carrying them? The prosecution made no case for this either.

That a case that begins with the possession of three letters can proceed all the way to judgement and conviction is alarming. It tears at the trust we all vest in our law-and-order mechanisms: that they will act fairly and efficiently to deliver justice. This is a contract between governments and those they govern, the two-way articles of faith that give justice meaning.

Without that faith, there is no law and order, no justice.

In April 2011, Harsh Mander travelled to Dantewada in Chhattisgarh at the direction of the Supreme Court, to investigate an incident in which CRPF men burned down the houses in three villages. Mander's report to the Supreme Court is a window into the violence and what he calls 'vicious personalized hatred' that exists between the Maoists, on one hand, and the Salwa Judum operation and state authorities, on the other.

And yet that violence and hatred is not the real tragedy of Dantewada. As Mander describes it, that distinction belongs squarely to the villagers in the area, caught between the 'warring groups' and left with no recourse to justice. Indeed, they probably imagine there's no meaning left to the word.

These lines from his report:

> 'The villagers of the region live in unabated conditions of great fear, of violence, but also consequences of taking sides, or being seen to be taking sides, with each of these warring groups. They are condemned equally if they act or they do not act. They are called upon by visiting dalams or squads of Maoists militants to supply them food, uniforms and sanctuary. They frequently comply, whether out of active sympathy with their ideology of armed rebellion, or from fear and helplessness. It is hard to tell what motivates this support – and I believe it is not even relevant to ask – but their perceived Maoist support results in grave and exorable consequences for the local villagers. Many are jailed as Maoist sympathisers and languish

> for long periods in prison, without even the succour of national and international support and human rights backing as surged for Dr Binayak Sen. Security forces often camp in the villages, or march through these, and make similar claims on the impoverished local residents, grabbing their grain and livestock, and demanding that they cook for them and serve them. They also suffer bouts of brutal retaliatory violence from the Special Police Officers and vigilante civilian groups like the Salwa Judum, who unleash periodic violent attacks on local villagers with or without the active support of security forces.'[51]

Brutality from both sides, but these hapless villagers end up in jail 'as Maoist sympathisers'. When that happened to Sen, as Mander points out, an entire campaign was mounted to show support and demand his release. And Sen eventually did get bail: both during his trial and now while he appeals his life sentence. Who speaks for the villagers of Dantewada and elsewhere, who are jailed and languish there for being 'Maoist sympathisers'? Where will their bail come from? Why should they not get bail as a matter of right?

This injustice of justice is the most frightening issue that Sen's case raises. Because when large numbers of people begin to feel like they cannot and will not get justice, there's a bomb ticking somewhere.

Security

No less a person than Manmohan Singh, India's Prime Minister, has pronounced that 'Naxalism remains the biggest internal security challenge facing our country.'[52] To varying degrees, many others agree with this assessment.

For example, Ajai Sahni, the Executive Director of Delhi's Institute for Conflict Management, has often written about security. While recognizing the threats to India's security, he also makes the point that a feeling of security comes from the hard work of bolstering our ability to fight the threats to it. 'What we see in the Binayak Sen case,' he wrote once, 'are politicians and policemen in search of symbolic quick fixes, unwilling to go the necessary and difficult distance to build the capacities to fight the Maoists.'[53] When I met Sahni in his office a couple of months after he wrote those words, he expanded on them, speaking with passion of the foolishness of expecting understaffed, undereducated and undertrained forces to maintain security. Who is training these men in the fundamentals of counterinsurgency, before sending them into Maoist-dominated areas to fight highly motivated and probably better-trained men?

I tend to agree with such analysis. Given the violence and brutality Maoists now regularly resort to, it's obvious that a Prime Minister would see the threat they pose, as Singh does. Yet my agreement is not founded solely on the violence and brutality, bad as those are. After all, if Maoists slaughtered 74 CRPF men in Chhattisgarh in April 2010, other Indians slaughtered 56 villagers in Bihar's Laxmanpur-Bathe in January 1997. More Indians slaughtered 3000 fellow Indians in Delhi in 1984. Yet more Indians slaughtered about 1000 fellow Indians in Bombay in 1992–93. Still more Indians slaughtered upwards of 1000 people in Gujarat in 2002.

Violence is not the sole province of Maoists.

Why then do I believe that Maoists represent the greatest threat there is to India? Because, primarily, of the issues that – at least on paper, at least originally – they stood and fought for. Because there has been little or no sincere effort to address those issues. With that lack of effort, you breed dissatisfaction, discontent, and Maoists. Addressing all this constitutes, for me, the larger and fuller meaning of Sahni's 'difficult distance'.

There's, of course, poverty. Injustice. Ill-health. Poor or nonexistent education. Apathy. Lack of opportunity. Corruption. Poor and too often biased policing. Governments that do not listen, do not deliver. You see all this and more every day in the news, and you recognize that it builds resentment among many sections of Indians – tribal, rural or urban.

What makes lives secure? One answer is that it is just a matter of stamping out dissent and trouble makers, of defeating Maoists and militants; just a matter of strong and effective policing. But a more complete, more effective answer would mean a sincere effort to listen to the concerns of Indian citizens, to address them with as much sincerity.

If you look at security in that light, there is material to think about nearly every day. For example, I remember a small news item about building highways; specifically, building 'a total road network of 14,000 km in eight Maoist-dominated states by 2017'. But pay heed to what the report begins with: this road-building scheme is part of the Centre's 'effort to fight Maoist insurgency.'[54]

A welcome development, and yet this announcement raises two issues.

One, 14,000 km is not trivial (the same issue of the newspaper reports that the city of Bombay alone has 1900 km of roads [55]).So why have we waited till 2011 and beyond, 64 years and counting after Independence, to build these roads? And since we did not build them, among other things we did not do in those areas, is it any wonder that these areas are today 'Maoist-dominated'?

Though it's not as if the Maoists built the roads either. But the point is, if successive Indian administrations in these areas had actually built roads – and provided much else that the people there lack – they would likely not be 'Maoist-dominated' today.

Two, this is indeed the way to fight the Maoists, just by delivering on promises made, on tasks to be done. Sincerely done, this will starve Maoists of their support among ordinary Indians, simply because there will be no reason for them to turn to Maoists. Without support, the movement will inevitably shrivel and die. There's your restoration of security.

In other words, security is founded on much more than just thousands of paramilitary forces, or expensive arms. In the end, those are shells, ineffective if what's inside is hollow. Security is ultimately built on the lives people lead. If they are discontented about something, if their administrations or elected representatives are unable or unwilling to address that discontent, there's soil to nurture the rise of Maoists.

Looked at that way, there are plenty of other issues that must worry us, issues that cause distress to ordinary Indians every day. Addressing them – think of it – might just produce headlines similar to 'To fight Maoists, centre to build highways.'

There are the potholes on our roads every rainy season, which are never satisfactorily repaired. There's the absence of justice for so many Indian massacres, for example, Delhi 1984. Government-run primary health centres (PHCs) that don't run because they have no equipment or supplies or staff. Ration shops that refuse to supply, for whatever reason, what they are required to supply. Government offices where the staff is indifferent and rude even to seventy-eight-year-old women. (This has happened.) The UID process during which officials have refused to accept forms even after people have stood in line for five hours. (This has happened too.) Municipalities that regularly demolish homes in our cities. Roads and flyovers left unfinished for years, causing profound inconvenience. Malnutrition. Villagers resettled in model villages that have no electricity. The lack of sanitation, so widespread even today that there are reports[56] suggesting that women are now asking grooms for toilets before they agree to marriage: 'No toilet, no bride'.

In early 2011, Maoists in Orissa kidnapped a district collector and wanted several demands fulfilled before they would release him. One report about this situation[57] told us what some of these demands were:

> Apart from the (almost mandatory, in hostage situations) demand for prisoner-exchange, [there were] demands that have been made on behalf of marginalised communities in India. The Naxals ask for: Scheduled Tribe status for certain Andhra communities; the closure of the multi-purpose Polavaram irrigation project; *pattas* (record of rights) of dispossessed groups; irrigated water supply to two villages in Malkangiri; compensation to two villagers who claim to have been tortured while in state custody; compensation to farmers living in areas submerged by the Balimela reservoir; better governing laws for the out-of-control bauxite mining industry; and the minimum displacement of tribal groups – and their adequate compensation – when development projects close in on their existence.

We may not agree with all these demands, but what do they really speak of except what the writer called 'the failures of the Indian state placed in sharp relief'?

As always in making such lists, they could be far lengthier. But let's underline the reason for listing and remembering these issues: security emerges from how a society addresses these, and many others.

This may be the deepest lesson from Sen's case: a country's security is ultimately built on the quality of the lives its people lead.

Democracy

Too much is made by professional hand-wringers of various threats posed to democracy. Yet there are times when it serves to remind ourselves what democracy is, what it has come to mean and what it potentially can be. Maybe this is such a time. And if the Maoist movement forces the country to introspect on those lines, it will have done some good.

Are we a democracy because we hold regular elections?

It's a good question, because what we do well in India, and have done regularly for decades now, is hold elections. Peacefully respecting the result of elections, governments have either taken office or given up power. Not for us the sham of democracy they may practice in certain Middle Eastern or Latin American countries. This is a source of pride and a reason to claim a degree of superiority over them.

The one major attempt to shut down Indian democracy happened in 1975 and was called the Emergency. Luckily, it lasted less than two years. But remember that it ended only because Indira Gandhi miscalculated her public support and held elections, believing she would win. Instead, she was flung out of office. Had she not called for elections, our history might have been quite different.

But with that history, we can still ask: is democracy as we have known it in India really democracy? What constitutes democracy, after all? Elections? Freedoms? Rights?

The rise of the Maoists suggests that what makes a democracy one is its willingness to listen to every voice. Not necessarily follow what they suggest, but at least listen. Even if they are critical and especially if they dissent – a democracy listens to them nevertheless. It's the unwillingness to listen to a spectrum of voices that raises questions about democracy in India.

For example, a lot of Indians ask questions about dams and development – to do with displacement, resettlement, benefits, the environment and more. Fundamentally, they are saying, 'If you ask us to make sacrifices in the name of development, we expect that in return, our lives will turn out better. But if they become worse – as we have seen happen to others like us – is this really development?'

You can debate this, of course. You've heard it said that 'somebody has to sacrifice, after all'; or 'You can't keep people stuck in the nineteenth century, living in forests'; or 'We need power and roads and irrigation'; or 'The resettlement and rehabilitation package we are offering is the most generous ever seen in independent India.'

But even so, the question about development remains legitimate. Examples like Bokrakachhar make them so. A lot of Indians feel nobody is listening to them, that their concerns will be overridden, and their lives turned upside down. To understand this, all you need to do is travel to where we have built dams – or even to where a sanctuary is established – spend time among so-called 'project-affected people' and listen to them, look at the way they live. Truly listen, truly look.

Do that and you'll wonder, as I once did, why a village that is close enough to see lights on a large dam on the Narmada, and in a small town that gets its electricity from that dam, itself sits in darkness years after the dam is complete. You'll know, as I did, the story in Bokrakachhar that cannot be rationalized. Dozens of families have been moved from their homes to a new settlement that has no health clinic, no school, not even electricity even though the new homes have wires and switches.

Should we listen to people who say, mindful of the experiences of others like them, that they don't want to move? And if we listen, how should we respond? Should we find some other route to development – divert the highway, or search for other ways to generate electricity – that keeps them where they are? Or should we make it a priority, a marker of this idea we call development, that if they move they will end up with lives better than they had?

Sen's case brings into focus themes like these. Leave aside the Maoists. Are we willing to ask and answer these questions about ordinary Indians? Would listening and responding to them signal a greater fidelity to the ideals of democracy than we have managed so far?

16

Doctor Only in Name

In December 2011, the students of Bombay's Sophia College organized 'Munsophical 2011', their first-ever Model United Nations conference. Popular among high-school and college students, MUN conferences are where they learn what diplomacy and negotiation mean. They break into teams that model the deliberations of the UN's Security Council, the Economic and Social Council and others. This inaugural Munsophical also had workshops on conflict resolution and international relations.

Attending the conference at Sophia were over a hundred delegates from colleges all over India, like the Madras Christian College, IIT-Kanpur and Symbiosis Institute in Pune. They also invited Binayak Sen, twice. One morning, he gave a valedictory address to the workshop on international relations. At the closing ceremony of the conference the next day, he spoke on 'The Idea of Human Rights'.

Sen explained that the idea that we humans are entitled to certain inalienable rights is a historically recent one. To make this point, Sen spoke about the sixteenth-century Spanish priest Bartolome de las Casas. When las Casas arrived on Hispaniola island (split today between Haiti and the Dominican Republic) in 1508, the local population there was about 60,000. 'From 1494 to 1508,' he later wrote, 'over three million people had perished from war, slavery, and the mines. Who in future generations will believe this? I myself writing it as a knowledgeable eyewitness can hardly believe it.'

In the sixteenth century, Sen said, nobody cared about such things as human rights. Today, decimating a population like the Spaniards did then is inconceivable, because we understand and covenant that as human beings, we have certain inalienable rights. The easy acceptance of atrocities as a price of progress, Sen said, is a thing of the past: humanity has 'learned a sense of moral proportion.'

Sen then connected human rights, as he has done elsewhere, to malnutrition and BMI. There was also a spirited discussion with the assembled students, including some questions that were, if not hostile, at least critical of Sen's views on development and security.

Going by the reactions and questions from the audience, this was certainly a thought-provoking session. But this is not meant solely to recount a stimulating encounter with several dozen MUN delegates. In the months since Sen's Supreme Court-ordered release on bail in April 2011, he has travelled around his country and outside to give talks and engage audiences. Besides Sophia, he has spoken in Tamil

Nadu, at AIIMS in New Delhi, in Jaipur, Seoul, Jamkhed in Maharashtra, at a Rotary Club meeting in Bombay, at the Ernakulam Law College and several other places. In an ironic echo of his inadvertent courtroom brush with ISI, he even visited the Indian Social Institute's Bangalore campus. Most often, he speaks of the connections he sees between development, medicine, justice, malnutrition and human rights. The lecture at Sophia, then, was typical.

To people who know him, this treadmill of travel and lectures is completely unfamiliar. In his pre-trial life, there was his clinical practice, his work with Rupantar and the PUCL, and that left time for little else.

'What about your clinical work?' I've asked Sen a few times. 'Now that you're out on bail, can you to return to your work as a doctor? Can you run the clinic at Bagrumnala?'

No, said Sen.

When Sen was out on bail during his trial, in 2009 and 2010, he visited Bagrumnala several times to run his clinic. After his release on bail in April 2011, he went there twice more. Each time, the police arrived soon after he did. They visited the families he treated and interrogated them for any 'links' to Sen and, by inferred extension, to Maoists. Clearly there are local informers who alert the police when Sen reaches Bagrumnala. This makes it difficult to do any worthwhile work there. It's not that the villagers don't want him back: his clinic was, after all, their only reasonable access to health care. He has discussed it with them, searching for a way to resume the clinic. But the attention from the police is an unwelcome burden, and after seeing it happen a few times, Sen is understandably reluctant to subject his patients to it again. As he told me the first time we met: 'I don't want to put pressure on the villagers there.'

What about practising medicine somewhere else? As Ilina Sen said once: 'Anywhere in Chhattisgarh, nobody will touch him with a barge pole.' In another state, it would be like starting all over again: find a place to stay, set up a practice, attract patients, build a reputation. Not impossible, but difficult.

The upshot: being a doctor is, in effect, a thing of the past. Sen was seeing patients in Bagrumnala, prescribing drugs and treatment, until days before his arrest in May 2007. For this graduate of the Christian Medical College in Vellore, this doctor with nearly four decades' experience in hospitals, that whole side to his life is gone.

During his trial, the Chhattisgarh Government asserted that 'Dr Binayak Sen is a doctor only by name, there is no treatment.' In the face of evidence of his work as a doctor – the records of treatment in Bagrumnala, for example – that was clearly untrue. Ironically, now that he has been tried, sentenced, jailed and released on bail, there is indeed no treatment that Sen does any more. His practice has indeed been reduced to the zero that the prosecution also claimed it was then.

Sen's work with the PUCL, both nationally and with the Chhattisgarh chapter, continues. Still, he has not been part, as he regularly used to be, of various fact-finding teams. That would rub too many people the wrong way. So now he helps plan the PUCL's activities.

Mindful of the incident in Raipur when a man in a jeep reversed to stop and stare at Sen, I've often wondered what it must be like for Sen to live in this climate. In a state – in a country – where you have a home and have built a life over many years, you suddenly find posters asking for your execution. You find people looking suspiciously at you. There are protest demonstrations outside places where you are to speak. You realize that police informers are not just to be found in books: they exist and some of them are informing the police about you. How do you live a normal life surrounded by all this? How do the Sens see all this?

'It's a really schizophrenic situation', Ilina Sen once said to me. She remembers people coming up to her husband at the Raipur airport to say: 'We're so happy to meet you! Please keep up your fight!' Many policemen are courteous and sympathetic to their situation. Sen himself mentioned a serving Army officer who approached him at the Delhi airport, saying how glad he was to meet a man he had long admired.

Yet to match that, said Ilina, they now realize they have no casual acquaintances any more. There are close friends, of course, people who will stand by them. There are also the critics and enemies, whom there's no way to reach. But the people you might meet on regular trips to the market, or a restaurant, people who might ordinarily stop to exchange small talk: those kinds of relationships, for the Sens, have 'ceased to exist'. People are wary, probably afraid of reactions from others, or perhaps the police. Consequently, they prefer to keep their distance.

Who will count the cost of all this – years in jail, yes, but also a career drowned, a life torn apart – if Sen wins his case in the High Court or the Supreme Court?

Speaking of the case. Sen was sentenced to life in prison in December 2010. This was because Justice Verma found him guilty of the charges under various sections of the law. This is well known, of course.

Specifically, Sen, Guha and Sanyal were convicted for charges under Section 124(A) of the Indian Penal Code, read with Section 120(B) (sentence: life imprisonment and a Rs 5000 fine); Sections 8(1), 8(2), 8(3) and 8(5) of the Chhattisgarh Special Public Safety Act (sentences: 2 years, 1 year, 3 years and 5 years respectively, with total fines of Rs 4000); and Section 39(2) of the Unlawful Activities Prevention Act (sentence: 5 years, with a fine of Rs 1000). All sentences were to run concurrently.

What's not as well known is that Justice Verma also acquitted the accused of the charges made against them under other sections of the law. Specifically again, these were: Section 121(A) of the IPC; Sections 10(A), 21, 38(2) and 20 of the UAPA. These deal with the attempt to wage war against the Indian state.

As Justice Verma observes about these charges:

> [I]t is not established that the accused persons were waging a war or trying to wage a war or abetting the waging of war against the Government of India or the State Government ... [I]t is also not established that the accused Piyush Guha and Dr Binayak Sen are members of some terrorist organization or group, involved in terrorist

activities, or crimes related to membership in a terrorist organization.

[T]he prosecution has failed to prove the allegation of crimes against [the three] under [these various sections of the law].

The judge acquitted the accused of charges under these sections. (Except for Narayan Sanyal, who was found guilty and convicted, in addition to the other convictions in this case, for crimes under Section 20 of the UAPA).

On February 28, 2011, just over two months after sentencing Sen to life in prison, and while he was still in prison, the state of Chhattisgarh filed an appeal against these acquittals in the Chhattisgarh High Court.

The interesting thing about this is how the state chose to inform Sen about this appeal, which of course they were legally obliged to do. That day, they handed a copy of their appeal to Sen in prison. Here was a man who was only allowed visitors once a month, meaning that's how often he met his family and lawyers. Other than that, he had no means to communicate with them. Therefore, it wasn't until Ilina visited her husband in the Raipur jail two weeks later, on 14 March 2011, that she and Sen's lawyers found out about this appeal.

As she wrote to several friends that day: 'Obviously we are under obligation to inform [the state] of our legal moves, but the state can get by with giving a copy to a person in prison who has no means of communicating anything to anybody.'

As I write this, both appeals (Sen's against his convictions, the state of Chhattisgarh's against his acquittals) are with the Chhattisgarh High Court. Neither has come up for hearing.

The doctor with four decades of experience remains a convict who is out on bail.

But if that's all right with you, give some thought to potential patients in and around Bagrumnala. For health care, they have to rely on the health workers who used to support Sen's clinic there. But if they need actual doctors, they must look elsewhere.

The diligent efforts of the state of Chhattisgarh have turned Sen, now, into exactly what they accused him of being in their charge sheet: a doctor only in name.

17

A Commentary

This book is not and never set out to be a biography of Binayak Sen. Nor is it an effort to paint him as a saintly man unjustly wronged. Nor a defence of Maoists. Nor an exhaustive line-by-line critique of the case against Sen – charge sheets to evidence to cross-examination to judgement. Nor a jeremiad about India.

What it is intended to be, instead, is an examination of the case against Sen, and its implications. It is an effort to understand the case and the issues it raises, in a wider context than just a courtroom. It hopes to make you ask this question: if the evidence presented against Sen is this flimsy, what does that say about the prosecution's own faith in its case?

In other words, if there was really substantial evidence against Sen about waging war against the country with the help of Maoists, why would the prosecution choose to insinuate as it did with the Mahila Kosh scheme?

Why would it claim that the mention of 'chimpanzee' by an acquaintance of the Sens is proof that the Sens are 'part of an international terror network'?

Why would it need to claim in its charge sheet that 'in terms of the practice of medicine [Sen] is a zero'?

Why not instead present the evidence against Sen?

But is there evidence against Sen? His friends and colleagues might claim he has a fine record as a doctor, but that cannot by itself absolve him of guilt. In the same way, the prosecution might claim that as a doctor he is a zero, but that too cannot by itself prove the charges against him.

What can prove the charges then? Evidence.

Is there evidence against Sen?

Ajai Sahni put it most pithily: 'The scandal of the Binayak Sen judgement is that the evidence against him is appallingly weak.'[58]

What Sahni means is that the evidence *presented in court* – that's all anyone can claim knowledge of – against Sen is appallingly weak. And yet if there was some astoundingly strong evidence against Sen available that's not already before the court, do you doubt that the prosecution would have presented it to the judge? Why have they not done so?

The answer is obvious. There is no stronger evidence against Sen. There is no evidence that he is guilty of the crimes he is accused of. It is inconceivable that any reasonable person would read the papers in this case – from charge sheets to evidence to judgement – and come to any conclusion other than this.

You want a final lesson from this case, an ultimate point this book makes? Try this: on 'appallingly weak' evidence – or let's be frank, on no evidence – a man has been sentenced to life in prison.

Try that for a commentary on India, a decade into the twenty-first.

Notes

1 *Ripples of Life*, CMC Vellore, December 2008.
2 Anjali Puri, 'The Gutsy Gang', *Outlook*, 25 December 2006. Available here: http://is.gd/OZakV0.
3 Syeda Hameed, 'The right prescription', *Hindustan Times*, 29 August 2007. Available here: http://is.gd/fT6iqg.
4 Minnie Vaid, *A Doctor to Defend: The Binayak Sen Story*, Rajpal & Sons, 2011.
5 Aman Sethi, 'We are walking in a state of famine', *The Hindu*, 19 April 2011. Available here: http://is.gd/OZIUPr.
6 Quoted by Manoj Mitta, "'Excesses' put Raman govt on defensive", *Times of India*, 31 March 2011. Available here: http://is.gd/2QynRb.
7 Order in Writ Petition (Civil) 250/2007, Supreme Court of India, 5 July 2011. Full text available here: http://supremecourtofindia.nic.in/outtoday/wc25007.pdf (PDF, 205K).
8 Essay reprinted in *Indian Doctor in Jail: The Story of Binayak Sen*, Doctors in Defence of Binayak Sen, Promilla & Co, New Delhi, 2008.
9 *Indian Doctor in Jail.*
10 *Indian Doctor in Jail.*
11 Transcript of Sen's Rotary speech and questions here: http://is.gd/L5DV40.

12 Video of Sen's interview with Chandra available here: http://is.gd/cjXpBj. This exchange starts at about the 2:30 mark on the clip.

13 Mark Bittman, 'Why We're Fasting', *New York Times*, 29 March 2011. Available here: http://is.gd/Zy2QtE.

14 'Armour of Goodness', *Outlook*, 26 May 2008. Available here: http://is.gd/gz81rw.

15 'Tomorrow it can be any one of us', *Frontline*, 28 January 2011. Available here: http://is.gd/PCTh5t.

16 People's Union for Civil Liberties, the organization founded by Jayaprakash Narayan to fight for civil rights during the Emergency of 1975-77.

17 'Barefoot Doctor', *Frontline*, 28 January 2011. Available here: http://is.gd/vv14BD.

18 Shoma Chaudhury, 'The Doctor, The State and a Sinister Case', *Tehelka*, 23 February 2008. Available here: http://is.gd/Y5d4j2.

19 At the Rotary meeting mentioned earlier, for example, the first questioner wanted Sen to 'elaborate the exact nature of his relationship with the Maoists'. Another wanted to know if 'it was the suspicion that he was treating Maoist patients that was the reason for his arrest' (see http://is.gd/L5DV40). And in a Pune meeting in September 2011, Sen 'said he had never supported Naxals or Maoists as he firmly believes in peace, justice and equality.' ('How can there be *sadbhavna* without justice?', *Hindustan Times*, 19 September 2011. Available here: http://is.gd/loYNde).

20 *Closing the Gap in a Generation: Health equity through action on the social determinants of health*, WHO, 2008. Available here: http://www.searo.who.int/LinkFiles/SDH_SDH_FinalReport.pdf (PDF, 7.3Mb).

21 What Virchow really said was this: 'Medicine is a social science and politics is nothing else but medicine on a large scale. Medicine as a social science, as the science of human beings, has the obligation to point out problems and to attempt their theoretical

solution; the politician, the practical anthropologist, must find the means for their actual solution.'

22 All three letters are parts of the charge sheet against Binayak Sen.

23 BBS Rajput and Team, Supplementary Charge sheet against Guha, Sen, and Sanyal, Police station Ganj, Raipur, 8 October 2008.

24 Order in Arup Bhuyan vs. State of Assam, Criminal Appeal No. 889/2007, 3 February 2011. Text of order available here: http://www.freebinayaksen.org/wp-content/2011/02/ArupBhuyanvsStateofAssam.pdf (PDF, 12Kb).

25 BBS Rajput, Supplementary Charge sheet against Guha, Sen and Sanyal, Police station Ganj, Raipur, 29 July 2009.

26 Photographs of these handwritten records are available at http://prabirkc.shutterfly.com/40

27 http://prabirkc.shutterfly.com/44

28 http://prabirkc.shutterfly.com/55

29 The order in its original Hindi, as well as an English translation, are reproduced in *Indian Doctor in Jail.*

30 'Farce in Court', *The Hindu*, 16 December 2010. Available here: http://is.gd/FCZH1l.

31 Both quotes from 'From White House to ISI, prosecution casts wide net', *The Hindu*, 12 December 2010. Available here: http://is.gd/YtCYS1.

32 See http://chhattisgarh.nic.in/schemes/mahila_kosh.htm.

33 'Malegaon blast case: Bombay high court restores MCOCA against Sadhvi, others', *DNA*, 19 July 2010. Available here: http://is.gd/UPOzAu.

34 N.C. Saxena, *Third Report of the Commissioner to the Supreme Court*, in WP (Civil) 196 of 2001 (PUCL vs Union of India and Others), 1 May 2003. Available here: http://sccommissioners.org/Reports/Reports/SCC3_0503.pdf (PDF 414Kb)

35 *2010 Global Hunger Index*, IFPRI. Available for download here:

http://www.ifpri.org/publication/2010-global-hunger-index (PDF 4Mb). Repeated in *2011 Global Hunger Index*. Available for download here: http://www.ifpri.org/publication/2011-global-hunger-index (PDF 3.8Mb).

36 D.K. and K.N. Agarwal, *Physical growth in Indian affluent children*, Indian Pediatrics, April 1994, pp 377-413. Available here: http://www.indianpediatrics.net/apr1994/377.pdf (PDF 2.9Mb)

37 English translation of the judgement, with a pointer to the Hindi original, available here: http://www.binayaksen.net/2010/12/judgement-english/.

38 Kedar Nath Singh vs State of Bihar, Judgement in Criminal Appeal No. 169/1957, 20 January 1962. Available here: http://www.indiankanoon.org/doc/111867/

39 See his message and photo on his Ministry's website here: http://mphed.nic.in/Message.htm

40 The government's *Sarva Shiksha Abhiyan* used to support 'alternate schooling facilities' under the Education Guarantee Scheme and Alternative and Innovative Education rubrics. In 2004, Rupantar applied for a grant to run such a facility. With the recent Right To Education in place, such facilities are now being 'upgraded' and 'mainstreamed'. See especially page 14 in the SSA document here: http://is.gd/jwozyU.

41 Omar Asghar Khan was a Pakistani economist and social scientist, and briefly a minister under General Musharraf. He died at the age of 48 in 2002. See http://en.wikipedia.org/wiki/Omar_Asghar_Khan

42 Example published here: http://www.counterpunch.org/arar11062003.html

43 Available here: http://is.gd/7hbH3k.

44 See http://www.cbc.ca/news/canada/story/2007/01/26/harper-apology.html

45 Ramachandra Guha, 'A Thousand Binayak Sens', *The Telegraph*, 23 April 2011. Available here: http://is.gd/Zj9pwm.

46 'Government calls Binayak Sen to draw health plan', *Hindustan Times*, 11 May 2011. Available here: http://is.gd/e6YmrY.

47 'Arundhati Roy's statement on possible sedition case', NDTV.com, 26 October 2010. Available here: http://is.gd/qodCJu.

48 Gautam Patel, 'Pasha of Politics, Caliphs of Culture', *Mumbai Mirror* and others, 8 July 2011. Available here: http://is.gd/smMbUO.

49 '*Ganiyari ke doctoron ke Naxali connection*', (Hindi), *Haribhumi*, 15 April 2011.

50 P. Zachariah, 'A Prize For the Prisoner', *Tehelka*, 3 May 2008. Available here: http://is.gd/ZuwJ8T.

51 'Report of Special Commissioner to the Supreme Court in the CWP 196/2001 on his visit to village Morpalli in Dantewada, Bastar.', 6 April 2011. Available here: http://is.gd/TnSuFe (PDF, 112K).

52 Reported widely. See for example 'Naxalism remains biggest internal security challenge', *India Today*, 24 May 2010. Available here: http://is.gd/q0IaUg.

53 'Guilty before being proven guilty', *Hindustan Times*, 1 January 2011. Available here: http://is.gd/e9inxg.

54 'To fight Maoists, centre to build highways at cost of Rs 10,000 crore', *Hindustan Times*, 8 August 2011. Available here: http://is.gd/5qk2ft.

55 '48-hr deadline ends, potholes still remain', *Hindustan Times*, 8 August 2011. Available here: http://is.gd/olML3o.

56 For example, Harmeet Shah Singh, 'In India's villages: No toilet, no bride', CNN, 29 October 2009. Available here: http://is.gd/QTYHM2.

57 Prayaag Akbar, 'Collector faced Prisoners' Dilemma', *The Sunday Guardian*, 27 February 2011. Available here: http://is.gd/3OinI4.

58 'Guilty before being proven guilty', *Hindustan Times*, 1 January 2011. Available here: http://is.gd/e9inxg.

Appendix 1: Timeline

2007

14 May: Initial arrest, Raipur

19 May: Raipur home searched. Documents and computer seized.

July–August: Charge sheets filed against Sen

7 August: Chhattisgarh High Court rejects bail.

November–early December: Arguments prior to charges. Charges are filed.

10 December: Supreme Court rejects bail.

2008

8 January: Trial begins.

Later that month: Secondary charge sheet (supplementary charge sheet) filed.

December: Chhattisgarh High Court rejects bail a second time.

2009

25 May: Supreme Court grants bail.
Trial continues.
September: Piyush Guha's bail application in the Supreme Court.

2010

Chhattisgarh High Court orders 'fast-tracking' of evidence, directs that the trial should be complete by January 2011.
24 December: Guilty verdict pronounced on several charges. The sentence: life imprisonment for Sen and his two co-accused. Sen goes back to prison. (Note that they are also acquitted of charges under several charges.)

2011

7 January: Appeal against conviction filed.
24–25 January: Hearings on suspending the sentence.
10 February: Chhattisgarh High Court denies bail.
28 February: State of Chhattisgarh files appeal against acquittals.
15 April: Supreme Court grants bail. Sen is released.

Both appeals (Sen, state of Chhattisgarh) are still waiting to be heard.

Acknowledgements

The Sen family. The doctors and staff at Jan Swasthya Sahyog, Ganiyari, and at Shaheed Hospital, Dalli-Rajhara. Sara Bhattacharji and Paul Zachariah at the Christian Medical College, Vellore. Lawyers in Bilaspur and New Delhi. Ajai Sahni. Aman Sethi. Viggy Row. Neela.

Ravi and Ramani. Vibha. A host of others for information, opinion, disagreement, discussion and support.

Thank you.